Excel for Fantasy Football

HOW TO BUILD

FANTASY FOOTBALL CHEAT SHEETS

WITH MICROSOFT EXCEL 2003 ™

John Broberg

www.lulu.com

If you purchase this book without a cover you should be aware that this book may have been stolen property and reported as "unsold and destroyed" to the publisher. In such case neither the author nor the publisher has received any payment for this "stripped book."

Copyright © 2011 by John Broberg

All rights reserved. Except as permitted under the U.S. Copyright Act of 1976, no part of this publication may be reproduced, distributed, or transmitted in any form or by any means, or stored in a database or retrieval system, without the prior written permission of the publisher.

www.lulu.com

Printed in the United Sates of America

First Edition: July 2011

10 9 8 7 6 5 4 3 2 1

Library of Congress Cataloging-in-publication Data

Broberg, John.

Excel for Fantasy Football; How to Build Fantasy Football Cheat Sheets with Microsoft Excel / John Broberg. – 1st ed.

p. cm.

Summary: "Learn to build your own fantasy football cheat sheets with Microsft Excel." -- Provided by the author

ISBN-13: 978-1-257-92321-2

1. Fantasy football (game) 2. Fantasy games. I. Title.

Table of Contents

Epilogue– Why Use Excel in Fantasy Football?.. 1

Introduction — It's a Numbers Game 2

Step 1 — Consume Mass Quantities (Import Fantasy Football Stats) 3

Step 2 — Assign Fantasy Points by Week 5

Step 3 — PivotTable! 7

Step 4 — VLOOKUP for 3 Seasons Fantasy Points 10

Step 5 — VLOOKUP for Last Season Fantasy Points 15

Step 6 — Blended RANK'arita (no salt) 16

Step 7 — CRANK It Up (Consistency RANKing of Fantasy Football Points) 21

Step 8 — Tiers for Fears 28

Epilogue– Why Use Excel in Fantasy Football?

With Auto-Pick and ready-made cheat sheets available, why waste time with an Excel spreadsheet, right? Well, Excel for Fantasy Football intends to teach Excel skills first and foremost, but in the fun context of fantasy football.

In my past job hunts, Excel skills were always a job requirement. As a hiring manager, I noticed that candidates' skill levels would make or break them, in the first interview. Today's office workers find it nearly impossible to succeed without at least some experience with MS Excel.

In particular, two Excel skills seem to set apart the experts from the novices — PivotTables and LOOKUP functions. Creating this book's fantasy football cheat sheet employs both skills.

Get job skills while playing fantasy football? Yes. That's the idea here.

Already have a job? Then, brand yourself as an Excel expert, and go for that promotion.

Introduction — It's a Numbers Game

Fantasy Football is about stats. That's it.

(Okay… it's also about drinking beer while watching and discussing football, and especially about trash-talking with friends and coworkers using terribly graphic metaphors of severe pain and humiliation that they will suffer from your ingenious lineup. But, I digress.)

In regards to the *mechanics* of fantasy football, weekly player stats are converted into fantasy points and then totaled.

Those totals determine who won their match-up.

Wins and Losses are tallied.

Teams with the most Wins advance to the playoffs.

However, let's remember that statistical analysis with Microsoft Excel is no substitute for *qualitative* judgment. Quantitative analysis simply organizes the massive amounts of data (NFL stats) into useful information. With this information, we can apply our judgment to make sound decisions. For example, which player to draft, when to draft him, and whom to start.

After all, we're attempting to predict the future performance of 300 different players over a 17 week period. Never mind that we get caught in the rain unprepared, and stuck in traffic. In fantasy football, we don't need to predict the future perfectly, just better than our opponents predict it. Do you think they are using PivotTables, VLOOKUP functions and blended RANKings for their draft? Probably not. But, you can, by following the steps in this book.

These steps will show you how to organize a mountain of NFL stats. (NFL stats are provided as a FREE download at excelfantasyfootball.wordpress.com). With these steps, you will tame that swirling sea of numbers into a detailed ranking of players for your draft. After applying your own judgment to the rankings, you will have built a powerfully customized cheat sheet of you own. Once completed, guard that cheat sheet with your life. You worked hard on it. Your opponents can make their own.

Although the following steps are applied to ranking QB's, the same process can be applied to RB's and WR's. I don't bother using this extensive ranking process with TE's, DEF's or K's; the return on effort is minimal, in my opinion.

Most importantly, if you're new to PivotTables and the VLOOKUP function, you will gain marketable **job skills** by following these steps. Yes, these skills are high in demand. And yes, you can put these skills on your resume. At your next job interview, should you volunteer that you gained your Excel skills by playing fantasy football? Maybe. Maybe not. As a hiring manager myself, I would have delighted in that fact. As for other hiring managers, proceed at your own risk.

Lastly, I've been working feverishly to get this manual ready for the 2011 season. As a result, I admit that minor errors remain, which I plan to correct by the next edition. I sincerely appreciate your patience and understanding. Moreover, I would appreciate your honest feedback. Feel free to contact me at my blog (excelfantasyfootball.wordpress.com), or by emailing me at john@upgradient.com. I look forward to hearing from you.

excelfantasyfootball.wordpress.com

Step 1 — Consume Mass Quantities (Import Fantasy Football Stats)

The Coneheads, from Saturday Night Live (1977), would "consume mass quantities," by gulping down entire six-packs and bags of chips. With the Excel spreadsheet, we can consume mass quantities of fantasy football stats, and properly digest this data into useful information for the big draft.

I only gather data of the last three seasons. Older data loses its value. Use less than three years worth of data, and we might as well pick players based on their last season's performance.

Since I'm in Yahoo! leagues, I stumbled across the Yahoo! statistics page. (You can find the link at excelfantasyfootball.wordpress.com.) It has all the basic elements needed to begin building our Excel spreadsheet (Yards, TD's, Fumbles, etc.).

First, filter the online data by Position, Year and Timeframe. Always set the Players filter to "All Players".

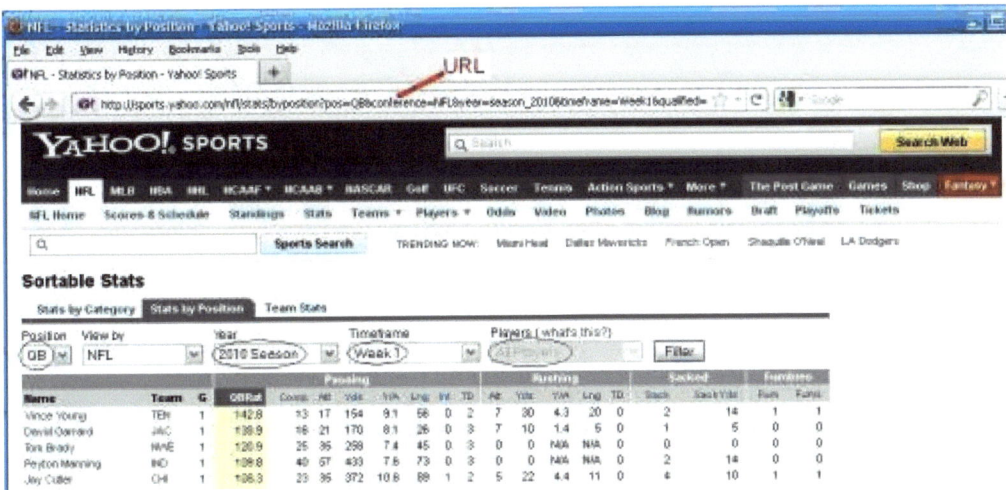

Import the raw data directly from the webpage by clicking Data → Import External Data → New Web Query, thus opening the Edit Web Query, as follows:

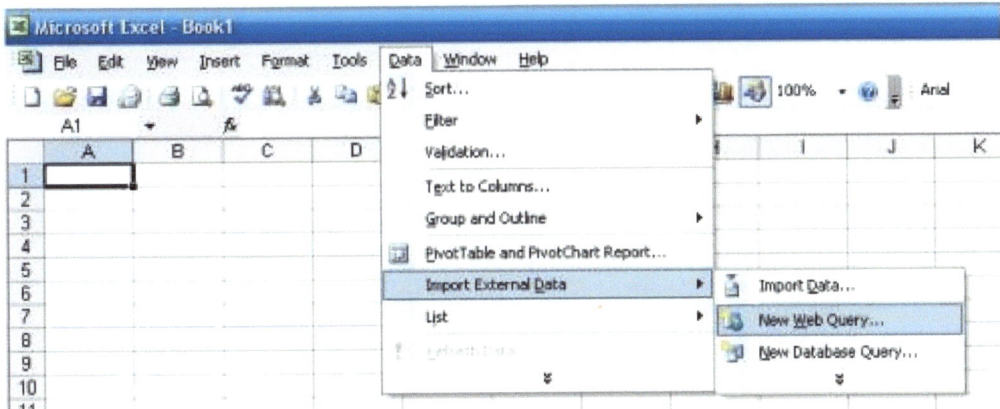

Copy the URL from your browser, and Paste it into the Address field. Then, select the data set by clicking the yellow arrow, turning it into a green check mark. Now, click Import.

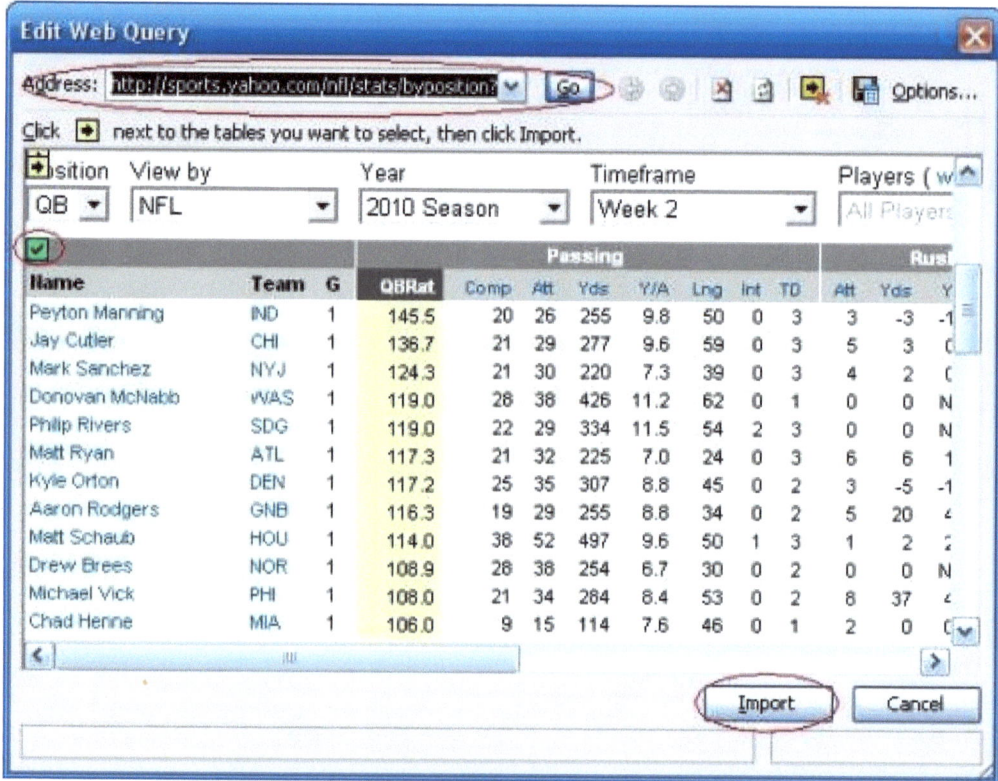

Your imported data should look like this on your Excel spreadsheet.

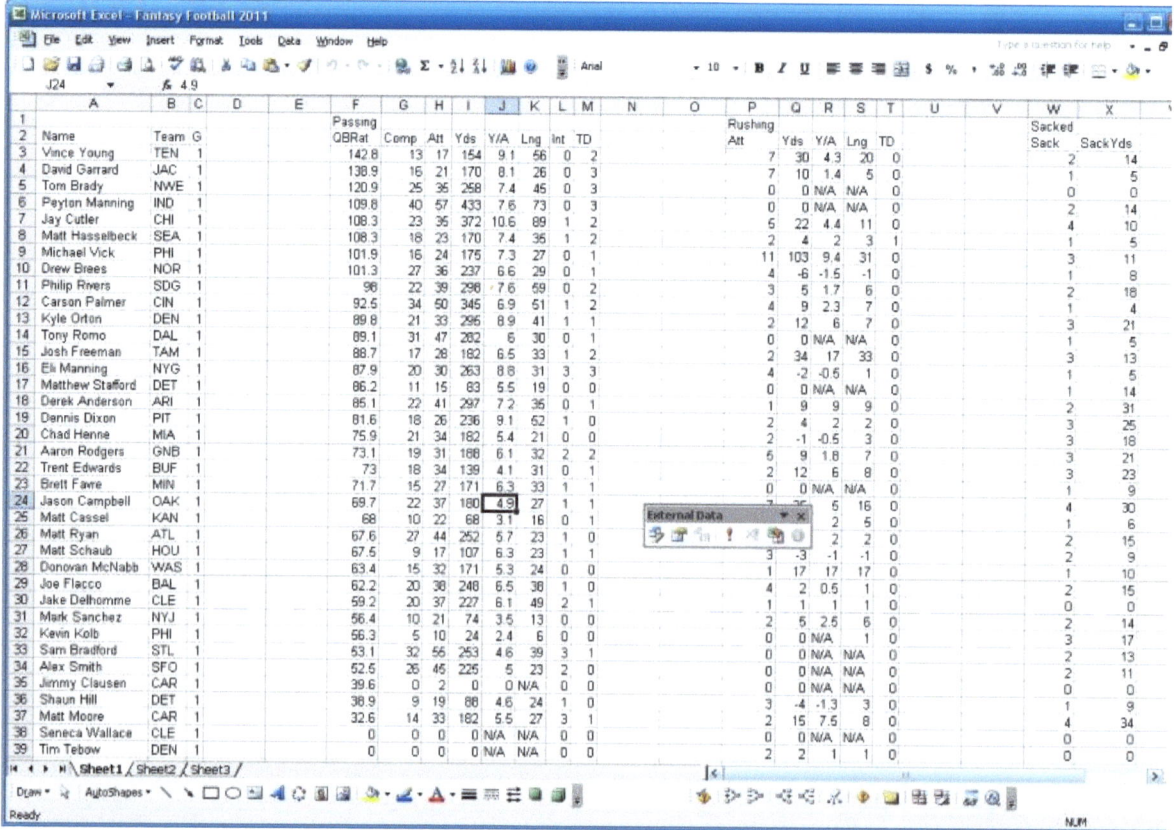

You can now repeat this step another 51 times (3 seasons x 17 weeks = 51 times), for each position. Yikes! **Or, just download the FREE NFL stats Excel spreadsheet from excelfantasyfootball.wordpress.com.** I have already done this tedious task for you. (This is my least favorite part of the process, too.)

Next, change the Games column header (G) to "Week", and add a column for the "Season" (e.g. 2010). (There's a nice blank column ready for you in column D. So, just type "Season" into D2.) Enter and copy the Week and Season for each player. This is key to creating PivotTables by Week and Season.

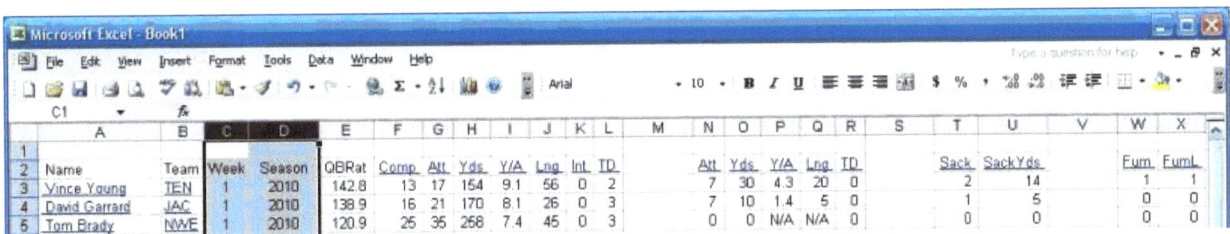

I like to categorize the data columns, in order to avoid confusion between Passing TD's and Rushing TD's, etc. Simply add detail to the column headers, such as Passing_Yds versus Rushing_Yds.

Now, we can clean up the data set by Deleting the excess columns.

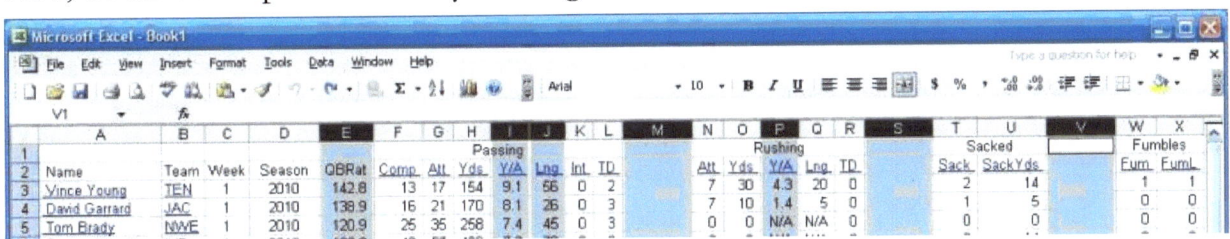

Did you really gather and scrub the entire data set yourself? You data-stud, you!

Step 2 — Assign Fantasy Points by Week

We now have data for each player's performance by week, over the past three seasons. We can now assign fantasy points to each player's performance by week.

We'll assume the following QB fantasy point scheme:

- 20 Passing_Yds = 1 point
- 1 Passing_TD = 6 points
- 1 Passing_Int = -1 point
- 10 Rushing_Yds = 1 point
- 1 Rushing_TD = 6 points
- 1 Fum_Loss = -1 point

(Naturally, you will want to use your own league's fantasy point scheme for your draft.)

Now, it's simply a matter of good old algebra. (I knew that we would use algebra after high-school; I just knew it!)

First, add the column header, Fan_Pts, to the right of your data set.

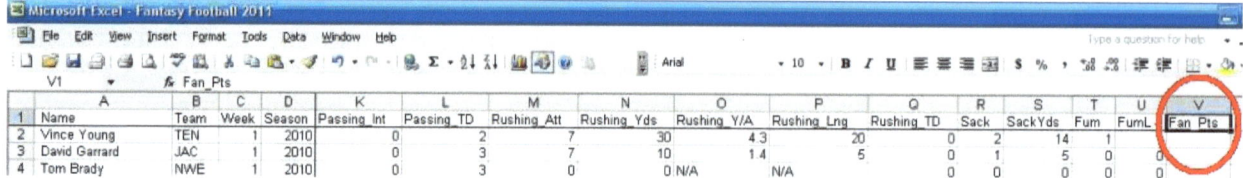

Then, create the following formula under the Fan_Pts header:

=H2/20+L2*6-K2+N2/10+Q2*6-U2 ← This formula translates the player's stats into fantasy points, based on the above fantasy point scheme.

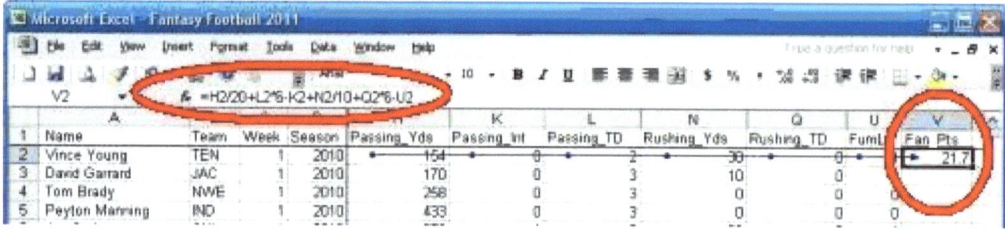

Now, double click the **fill handle**. (It's that little black dot on the lower right of the selected cell.) And, pow! You now have fantasy points by player, for each week of the last three seasons. I love that feature!

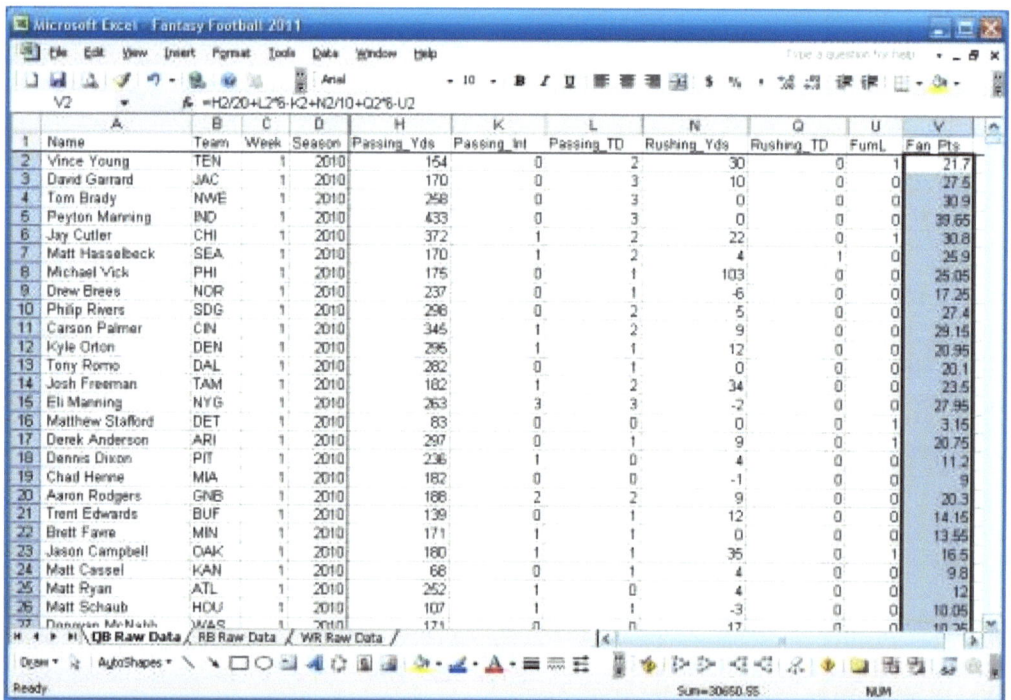

In Step 3, we'll begin the cool part — PivotTables. With PivotTables, we can convert the above data into more useful information. After that, we'll analyze further, making our way toward a fantasy football Excel cheat sheet... for the big Draft Day.

Step 3 — PivotTable!

Here's the big deal for this book: learning an Excel spreadsheet skill that separates the experts from the novices. PivotTables.

In this step, we get to learn PivotTables, while building our fantasy football cheat sheet!

Select any cell in the raw data table. Then, from the Data menu, select "PivotTable and PivotChart Report."

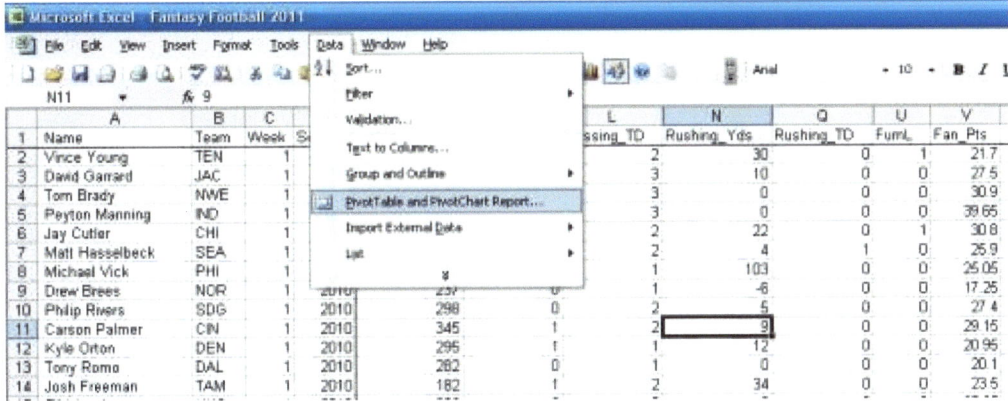

Click the following radio buttons, and then click Next:

Excel will automatically select the entire data range. So, just click Next.

Then, select "New Worksheet" for our PivotTable, and click Finish.

Double click the new tab, and change its title to "QB FP Year" as follows:

Now, from the PivotTable Field List, drag and drop the Name item into the "Drop Row Fields Here" section.

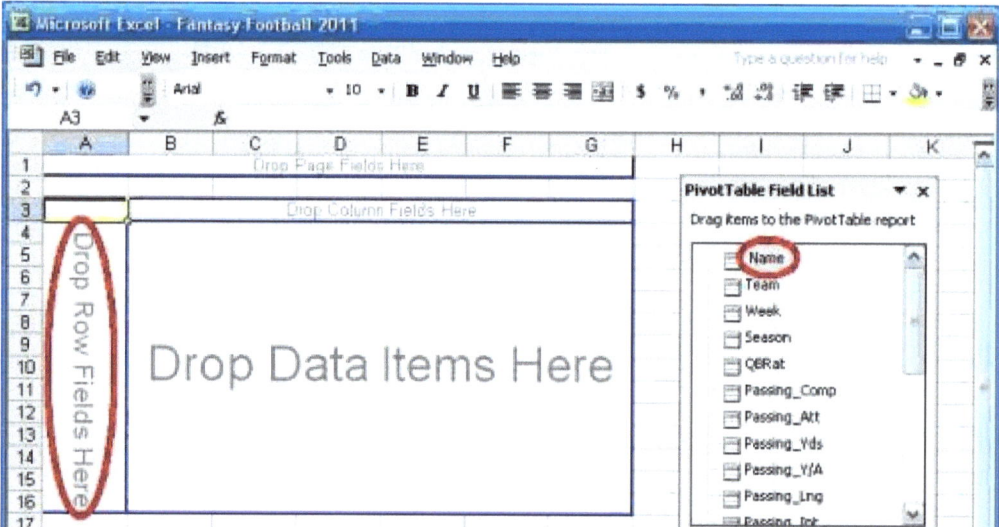

Next, drag and drop the Season item to the "Drop Column Fields Here" section.

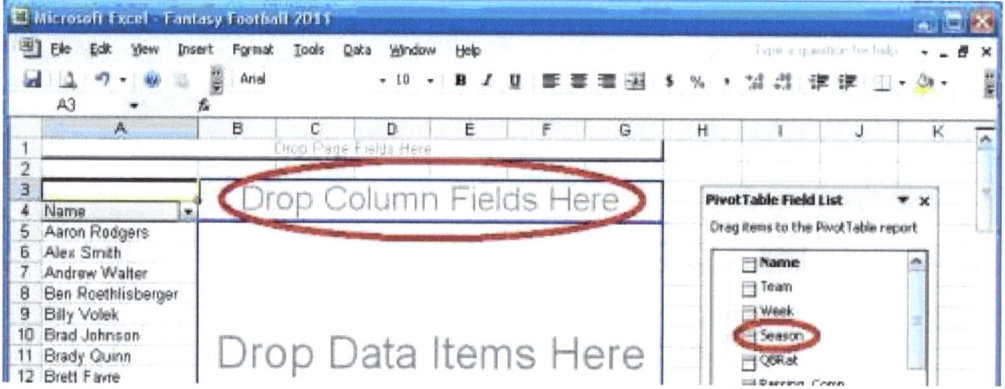

Scroll down on the PivotTable Field List, then drag and drop the "Fan_Pts" item to the "Drop Data Items Here" section.

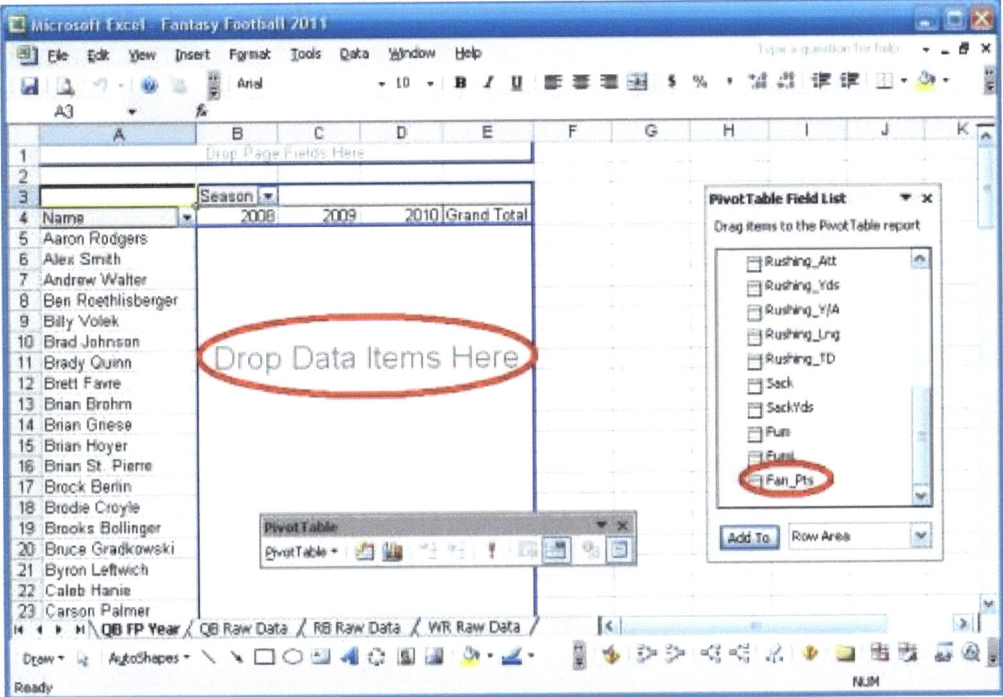

You've got a PivotTable!

Next to the Grand Total column, create an "Average" column, using the AVERAGE function for the three seasons. (Be careful not to include the Grand Total cell in your reference.) Double click the fill handle. And, pow! (I love doing that.)

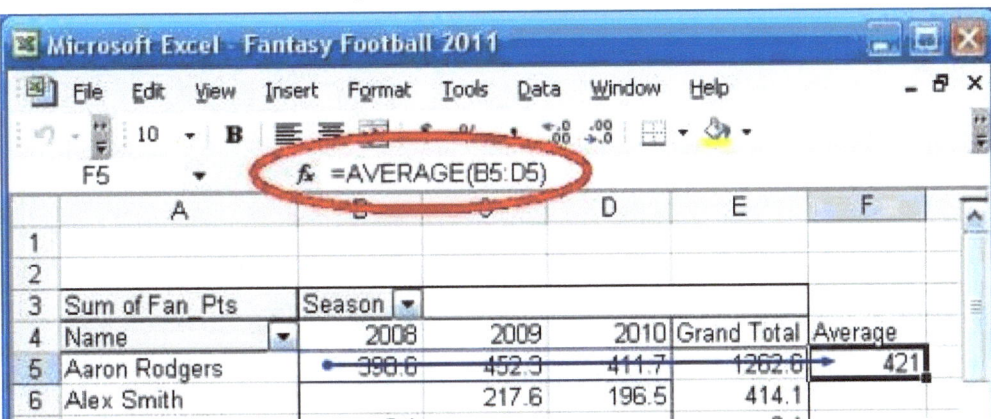

You now have average fantasy points by player, for the past three seasons. We can now rank players with this meaningful statistic.

		Season				
3	Sum of Fan_Pts					
4	Name	2008	2009	2010	Grand Total	Average
5	Aaron Rodgers	398.6	452.3	411.7	1262.6	421
6	Alex Smith		217.6	196.5	414.1	207
7	Andrew Walter	9.1			9.1	9
8	Ben Roethlisberger	267.15	377.6	283.6	928.35	309
9	Billy Volek		15.65	-0.1	15.55	8
10	Brad Johnson	28.25			28.25	28
11	Brady Quinn	38	120.75		158.75	79

Was this your first PivotTable? If so, congratulations! You just made a huge step from Excel novice toward Excel expert.

Step 4 — VLOOKUP for 3 Seasons Fantasy Points

With the raw fantasy football stats converted into a PivotTable, we can begin building our cheat sheet for the big draft.

First, create a new worksheet, by right-clicking a tab and selecting Insert. Select Worksheet in the Insert window, and click OK.

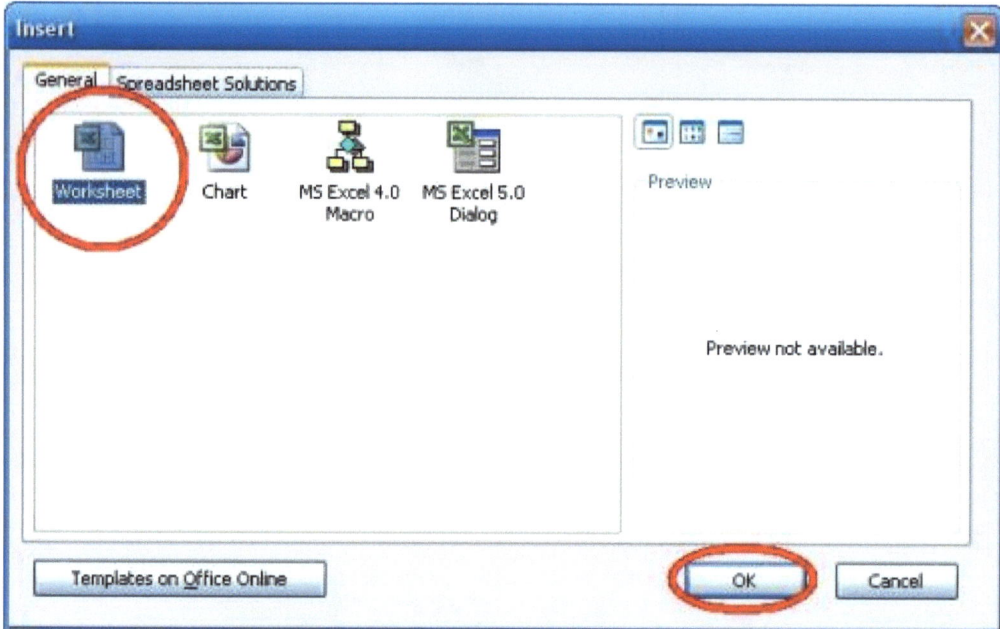

Double-click the tab of the new worksheet, and change its title to "QB_Cheat Sheet."

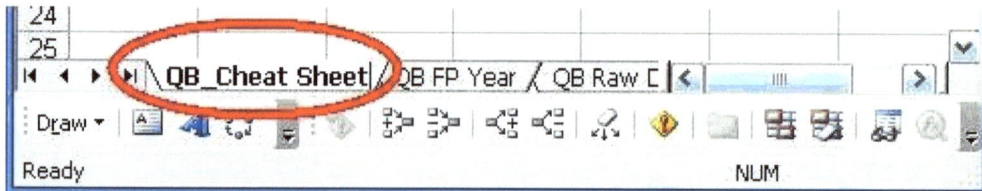

Now, we could Copy and Paste all of the QB's from the QB FP Year worksheet. However, that's over 100 QB's to consider (and I'm not really interested in Brock Berlin's performance on the field). Instead, I'll Copy and Paste only the *starting* QB's, using a depth chart from thehuddle.com.

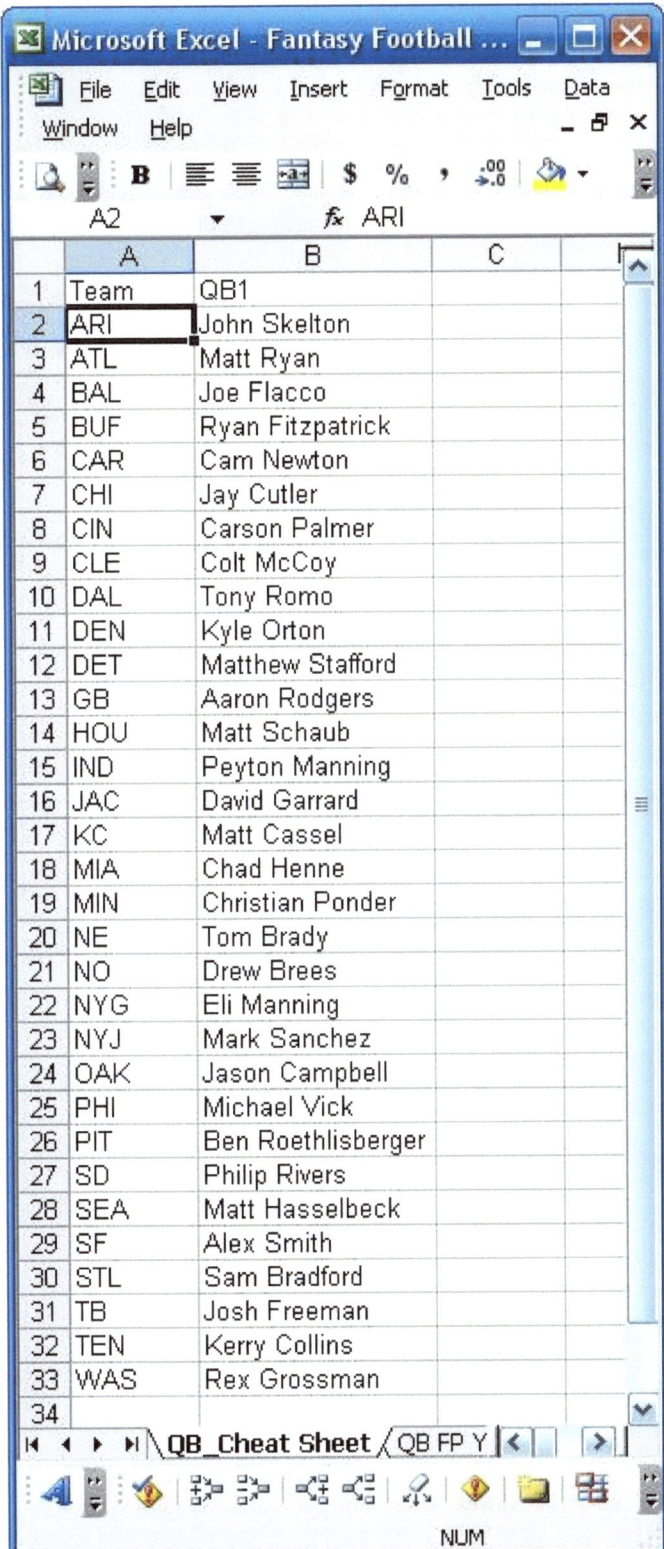

Type the column header, "Avg. FP/Yr.", into cell C1. Then, select cell C2, and click the function button.

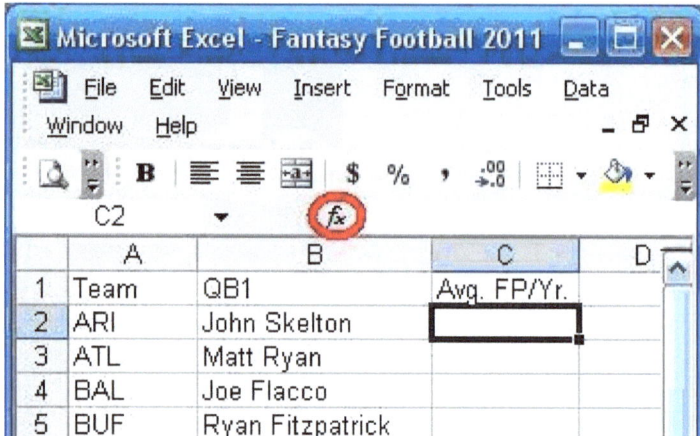

Type "vlookup" in the "Search for a function" field, and click Go. Select VLOOKUP. Then, click OK.

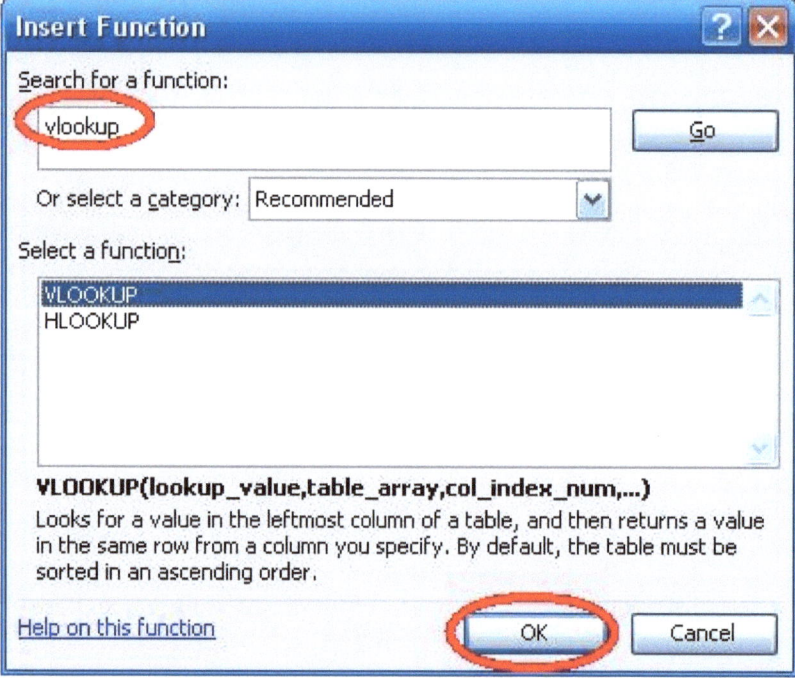

For the Lookup_value field in the Function Arguments window, select the corresponding QB's name. In this case, John Skelton (cell B2).

For the Table_array field, click the QB FP Year worksheet tab, and highlight the entire data range (including the Average column).

Enter "6" in the field for Col_index_num. This instructs the VLOOKUP function to return the corresponding value in the Average column, of the QB FP Year worksheet.

Type "false" into the Range_lookup field.   (Although optional, I like to ensure that the Lookup_value is an exact match.)

Click Ok.

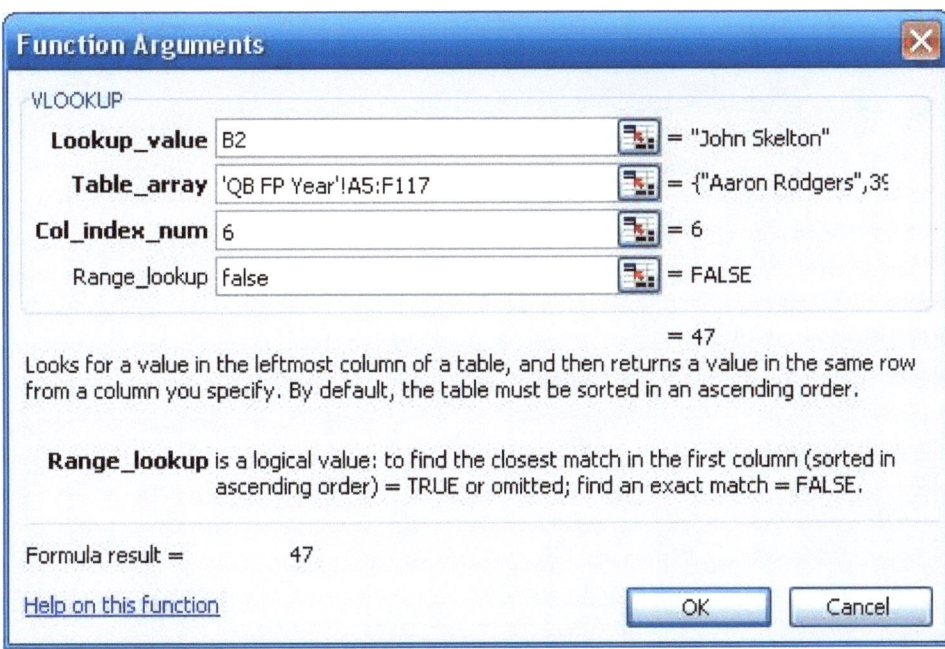

Insert "$" into your formula as follows (keeping our table reference static):

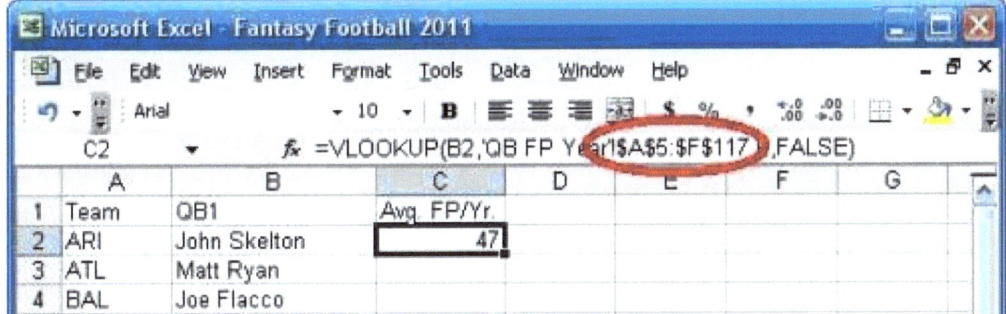

Click the fill handle again to copy the formula to the other QB's.

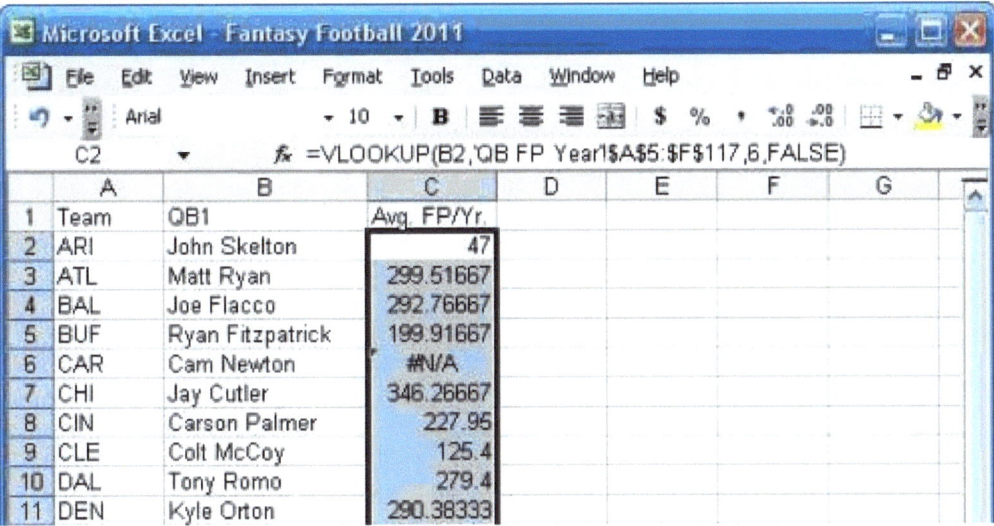

The Decrease Decimal button will clean up the formatting easily.

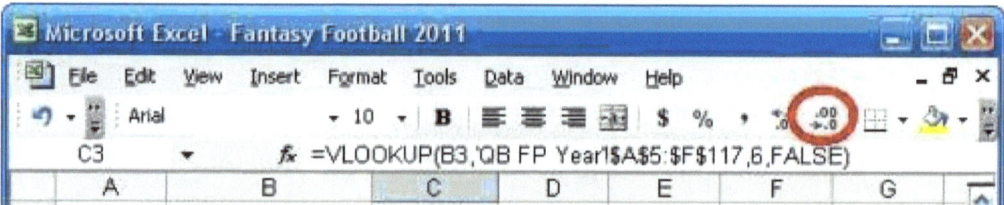

Cam Newton and Christian Ponder are rookies. Since I won't use a valuable draft spot on a rookie QB, I'll just enter zero for their values in place of "#NA."

Using the Sort feature, from the Data menu, we can arrange the QB's by order of average fantasy points.

Congratulations! You have used both PivotTables and VLOOKUP functions, while building your fantasy football cheat sheet. If you couldn't before, you can now say that you have "experience implementing PivotTables and LOOKUP's in Excel." You can even describe the process at your next job interview!

Step 5 — VLOOKUP for Last Season Fantasy Points

What?! Drew Brees outranks Aaron Rodgers?

Team	QB1	Avg. FP/Yr.
NO	Drew Brees	422
GB	Aaron Rodgers	421

Maybe, "back in the day"; but, surely the last two seasons' stats would challenge that result.

The following shows how Rodgers seems to be trending upward, while Brees is trending downward:

Sum of Fan_Pts	Season			
Name	2008	2009	2010	Average
Aaron Rodgers	399	452	412	421
Drew Brees	439	422	405	422

Their Avg. FP/Yr. shows that they've met in the middle, more or less.

So, we'll take this into account by weighting season 2010 more heavily.

On the right of the column header, "Avg. FP/Yr.", enter another column header, "2010 FP". Below that cell, insert another VLOOKUP function. This time, we'll use only season 2010 fantasy points, by entering 4 in Col_index_num, as follows:

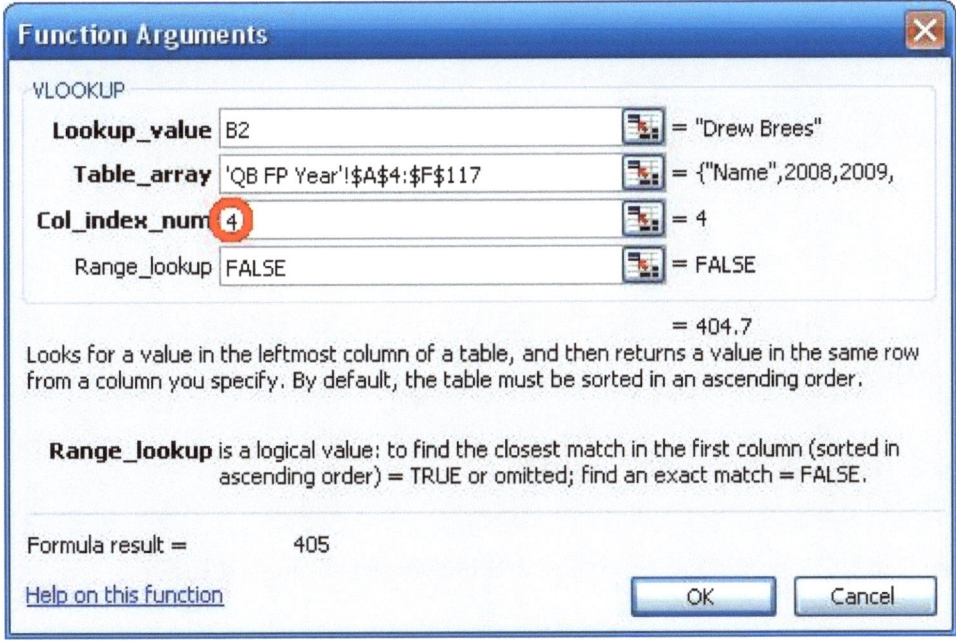

Remember to insert "$", in order to keep the range reference static when we copy the VLOOKUP to the other QB's.

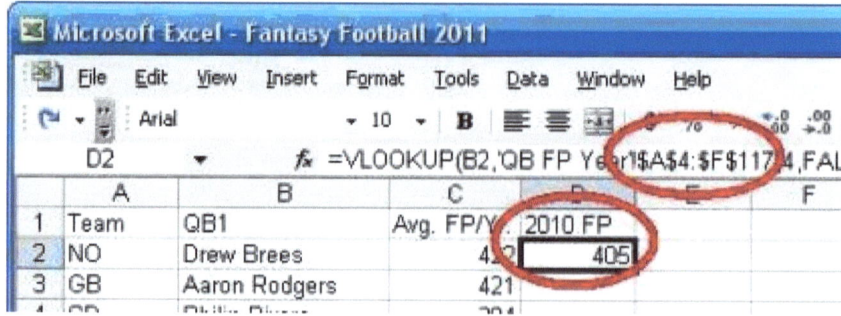

By double-clicking the auto-fill handle (my favorite feature), and zeroing out the rookies' results, we now have last season's fantasy points by QB.

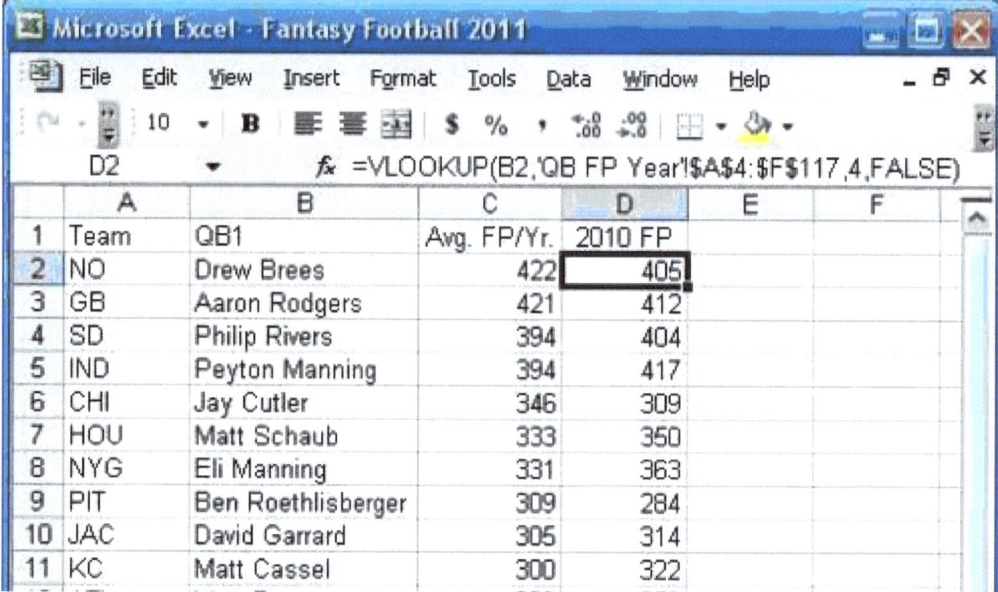

This allows us to weight season 2010 more heavily than the earlier seasons. We'll do that with the RANK feature, next in Step 6.

Step 6 — Blended RANK'arita (no salt)

Next, we're going to rank our QB's by fantasy points, with a heavier weighting on last season's performance.

First, create the following three column headers: Rank 3 Yr., Rank 2010, Blend.

16

Select the cell under "Rank 3 Yr." and click the "Insert Function" button (*fx*).

Type "rank" in the "Search for a function:" field, and click Go. Then, click OK.

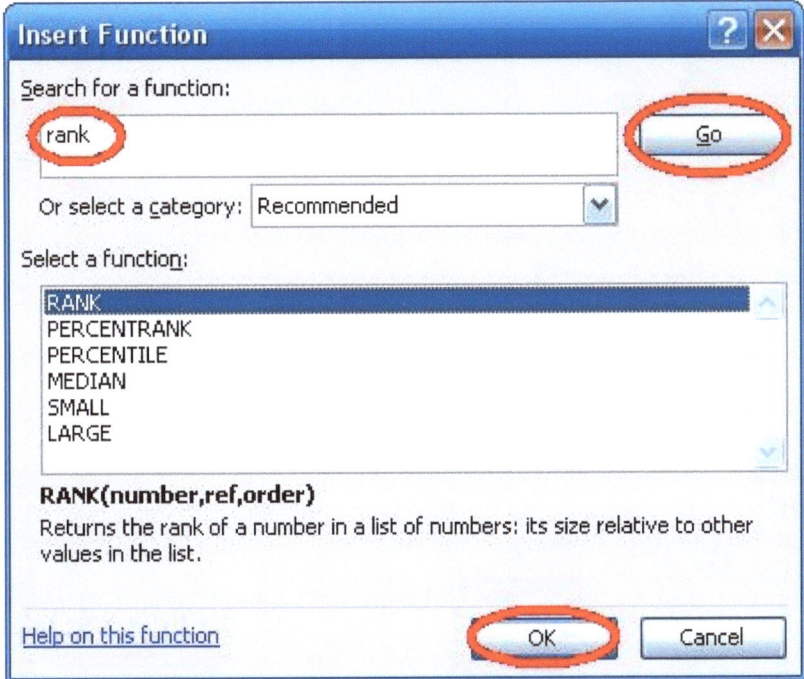

For the Number field, select the cell of the Avg. FP/Yr. for the corresponding player. In this case, C2 for Drew Brees.

Then, for the Ref field, select the entire range of values for Avg. FP/Yr. Now, click OK.

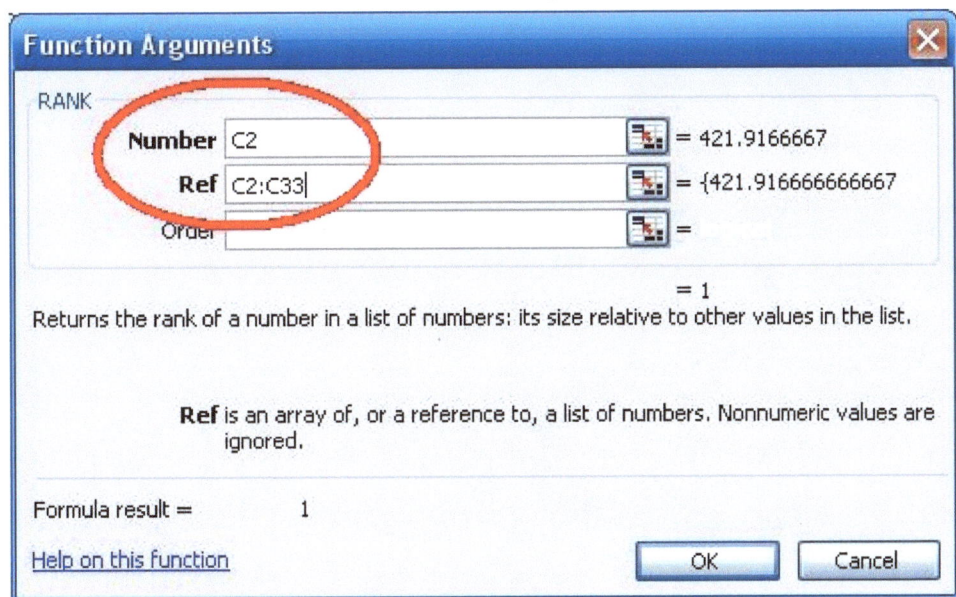

Remember to keep the range reference static by inserting "$" in the function, as follows:

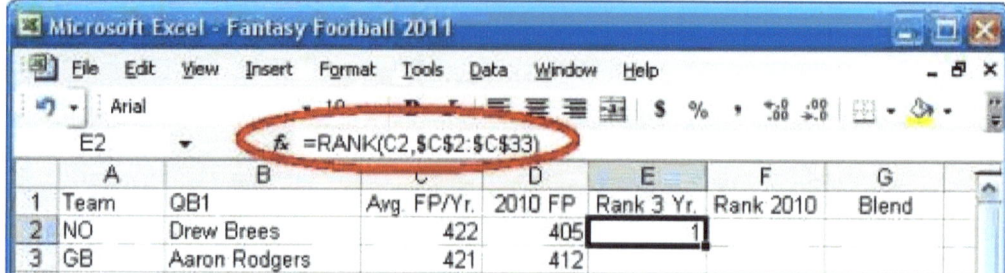

Now, you can copy the RANK function to the other QB's, by double-clicking the fill handle.

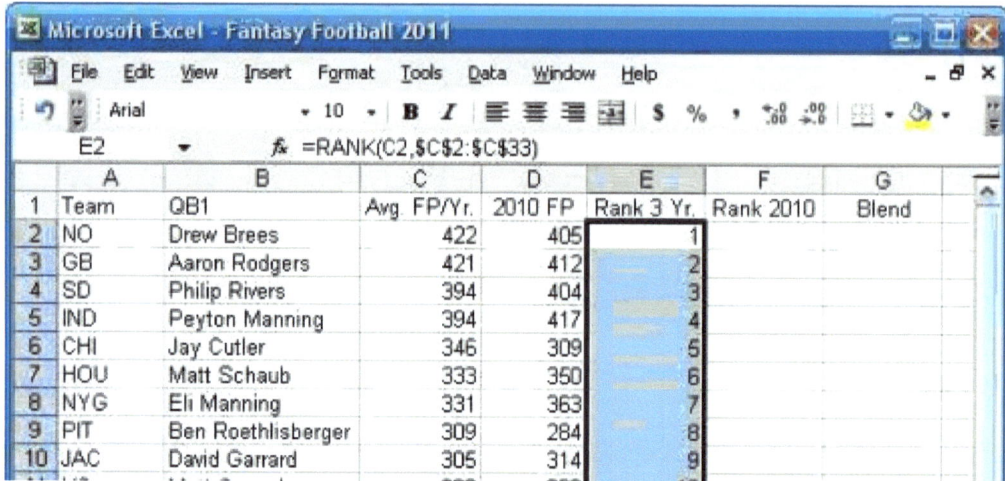

For the Rank 2010 column, repeat these steps, referencing the 2010 FP column.

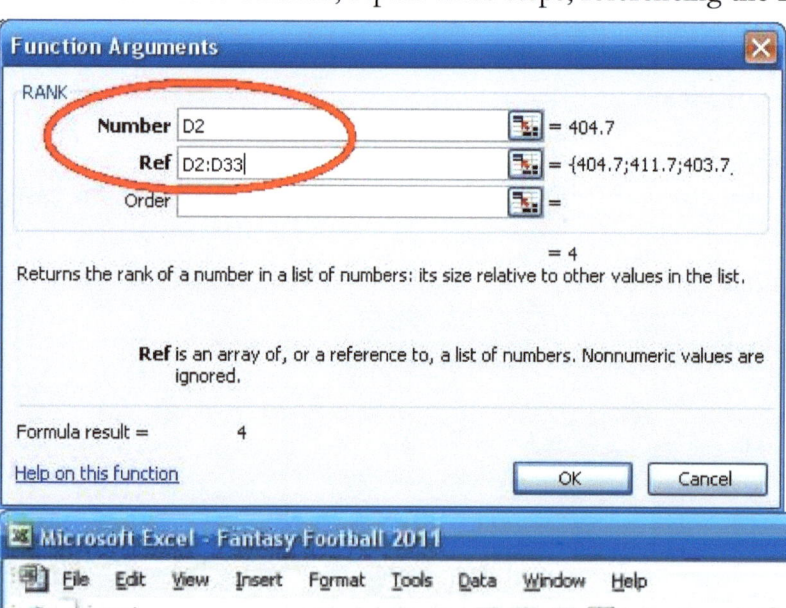

In order to blend the two rankings, we simply insert an AVERAGE function in the Blend column, as follows:

	A	B	C	D	E	F	G
1	Team	QB1	Avg. FP/Yr.	2010 FP	Rank 3 Yr.	Rank 2010	Blend
2	NO	Drew Brees	422	405	1	4	2.5
3	GB	Aaron Rodgers	421	412	2	3	

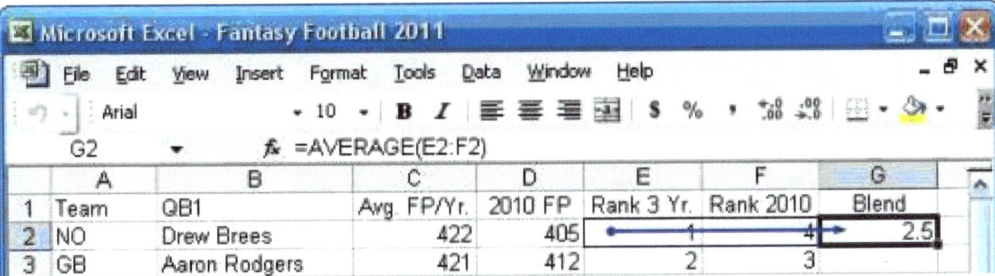

Auto-fill the column, by double clicking the fill-handle.

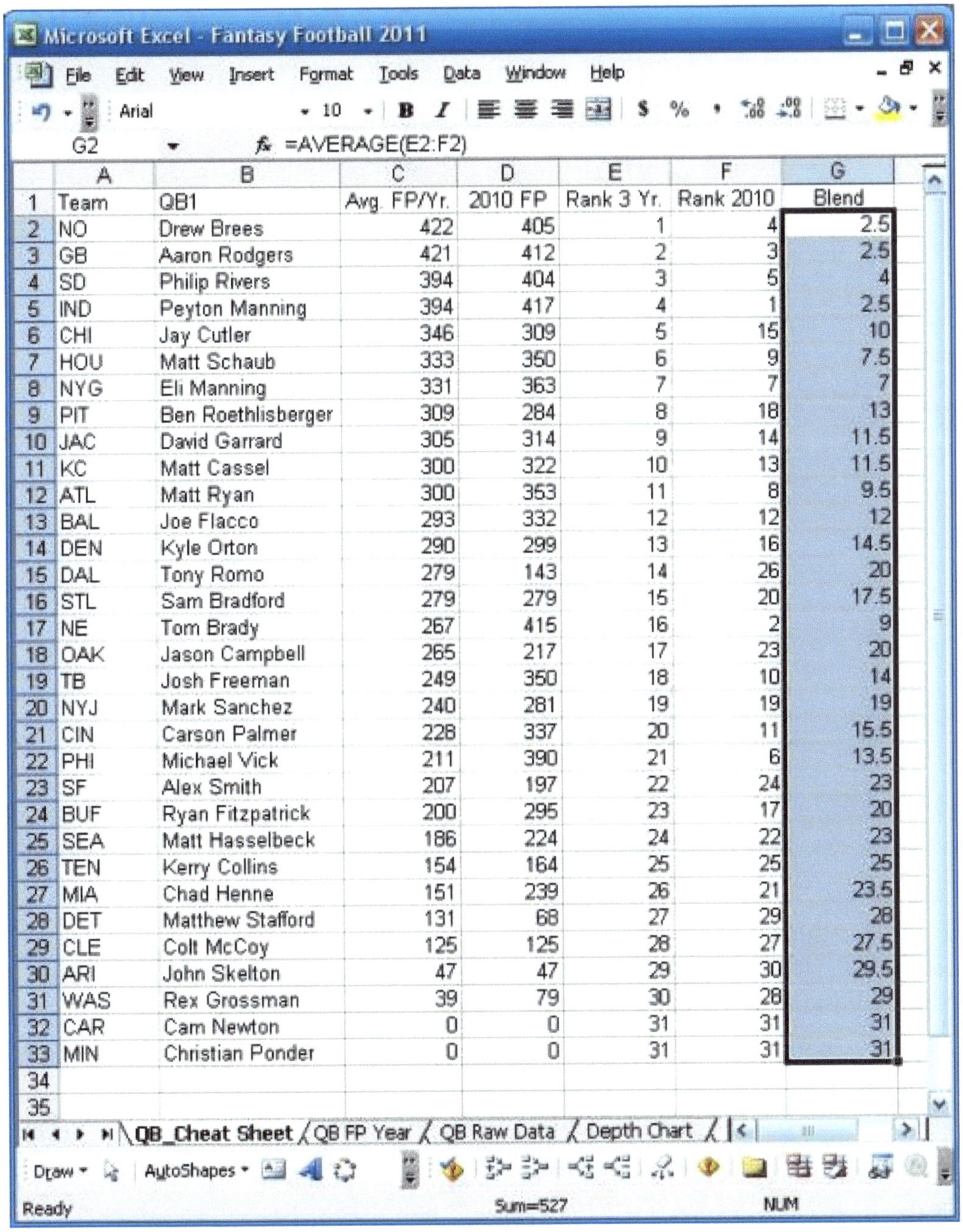

	A	B	C	D	E	F	G
1	Team	QB1	Avg. FP/Yr.	2010 FP	Rank 3 Yr.	Rank 2010	Blend
2	NO	Drew Brees	422	405	1	4	2.5
3	GB	Aaron Rodgers	421	412	2	3	2.5
4	SD	Philip Rivers	394	404	3	5	4
5	IND	Peyton Manning	394	417	4	1	2.5
6	CHI	Jay Cutler	346	309	5	15	10
7	HOU	Matt Schaub	333	350	6	9	7.5
8	NYG	Eli Manning	331	363	7	7	7
9	PIT	Ben Roethlisberger	309	284	8	18	13
10	JAC	David Garrard	305	314	9	14	11.5
11	KC	Matt Cassel	300	322	10	13	11.5
12	ATL	Matt Ryan	300	353	11	8	9.5
13	BAL	Joe Flacco	293	332	12	12	12
14	DEN	Kyle Orton	290	299	13	16	14.5
15	DAL	Tony Romo	279	143	14	26	20
16	STL	Sam Bradford	279	279	15	20	17.5
17	NE	Tom Brady	267	415	16	2	9
18	OAK	Jason Campbell	265	217	17	23	20
19	TB	Josh Freeman	249	350	18	10	14
20	NYJ	Mark Sanchez	240	281	19	19	19
21	CIN	Carson Palmer	228	337	20	11	15.5
22	PHI	Michael Vick	211	390	21	6	13.5
23	SF	Alex Smith	207	197	22	24	23
24	BUF	Ryan Fitzpatrick	200	295	23	17	20
25	SEA	Matt Hasselbeck	186	224	24	22	23
26	TEN	Kerry Collins	154	164	25	25	25
27	MIA	Chad Henne	151	239	26	21	23.5
28	DET	Matthew Stafford	131	68	27	29	28
29	CLE	Colt McCoy	125	125	28	27	27.5
30	ARI	John Skelton	47	47	29	30	29.5
31	WAS	Rex Grossman	39	79	30	28	29
32	CAR	Cam Newton	0	0	31	31	31
33	MIN	Christian Ponder	0	0	31	31	31
34							
35							

Now, we can Sort by the Blend column, giving us a ranking of QB fantasy point production weighted by last season.

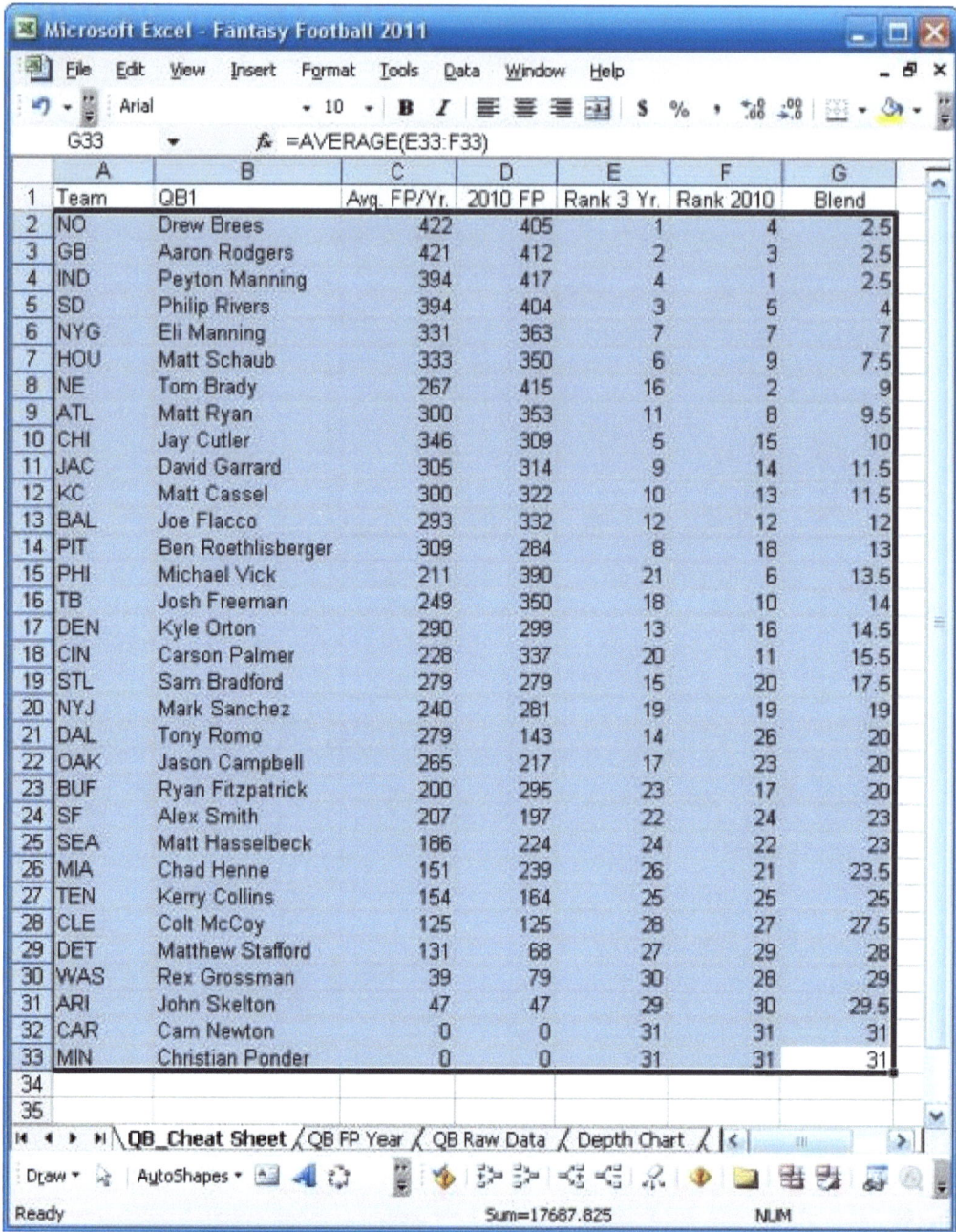

Uh oh… we now have three QB's tied for first, in the blended ranking (Blend column) — Drew Breez, Aaron Rodgers and Peyton Manning. This calls for my secret weapon. Consistency ranking. We'll use this additional metric to differentiate the players further.

I find consistency of fantasy point production just as important as total fantasy point production. I would rather have a player that produces an evenly consistent amount of fantasy points each week, than a player that produces many highs that are averaged with many lows.

This leads us to our next step – Consistency Ranking.

(As a side note, we'll naturally use our own qualitative judgment in the finalization of our cheat sheet. For example, Michael Vick's performance deserves a higher ranking, considering his time off (i.e. jail time).)

Step 7 — CRANK It Up (Consistency RANKing of Fantasy Football Points)

I would rather win more match-ups by narrow margins, than fewer match-ups by landslides. Remember, our overall Win-Loss record determines if we make it into the playoffs, not how badly we beat anyone. So, consistency of fantasy point production is just as important as total fantasy point production.

The following illustrates how consistent scoring can get you more wins than inconsistent scoring:

	Game 1	Game 2	Game 3	Total Pts	Wins
You	15	15	15	45	2
Opponent	10	20	14		
You	30	5	10	45	1
Opponent	10	20	14		

We can rank players' consistency, by comparing their median weekly scores for last season. We'll need to make a new PivotTable showing weekly fantasy points.

Yay! More PivotTable practice!

Select the QB Raw Data tab, and any cell in the array.

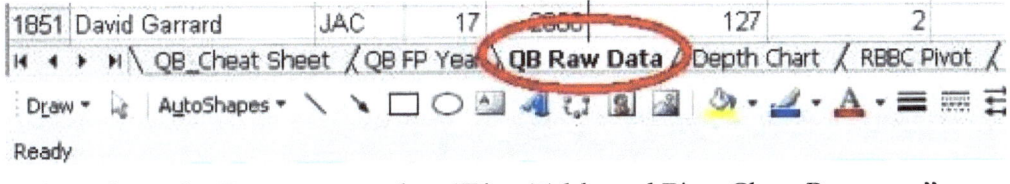

Then, from the Data menu, select "PivotTable and PivotChart Report…"

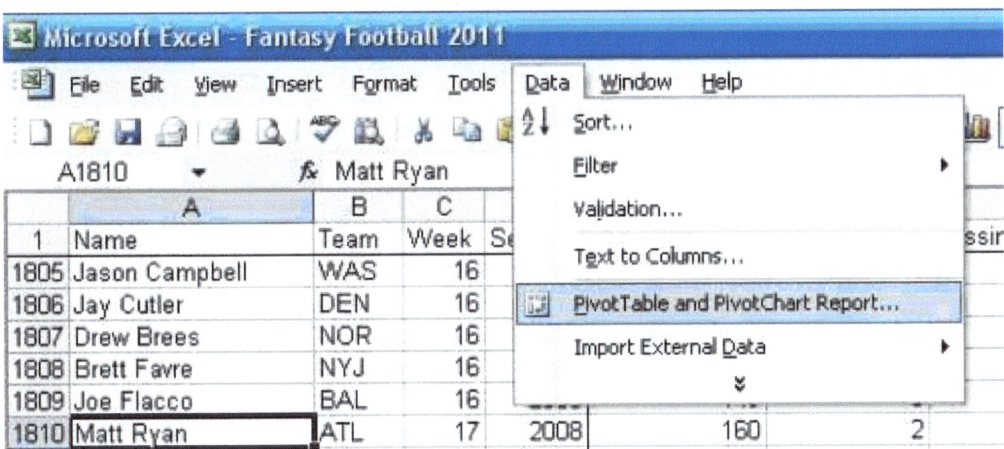

21

The PivotTable and PivotChart Wizard opens, with the default settings we want. So, just click Next.

The Wizard automatically selects the data range for us. So again, just click Next.

In this window, select Yes, as we want to save memory by reusing the same data.

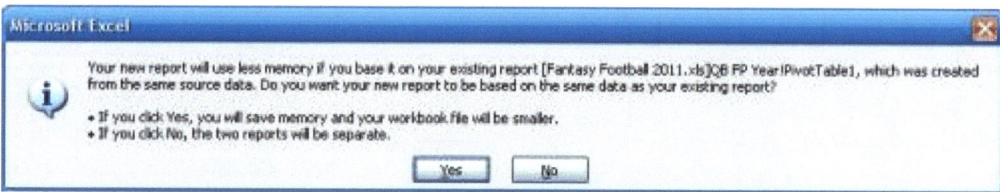

Make sure that the QB FP Year data is selected, and click Next.

We want a New worksheet for the new PivotTable. So, click Finish.

The new PivotTable will compare *weekly* fantasy points by player. So, do the following:

1. Drag and drop the Name item to the Row Field, of the PivotTable report
2. Drag and drop the Season item to the Page Field
3. Drag and drop the Week item to the Column Field
4. Drag and drop the Fan_Pts to the Data Items field

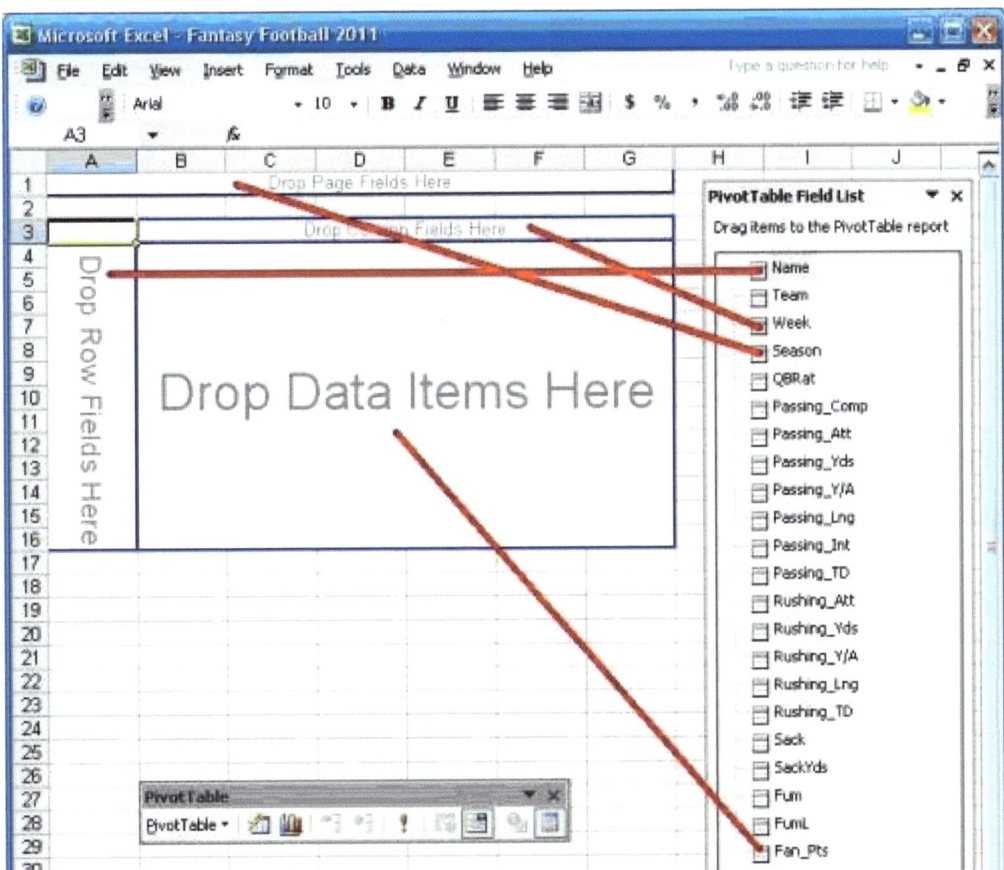

Yes! We have our PivotTable report…but, we're not quite there yet.

Let's isolate the PivotTable to last season's stats, by changing the Season page from (All) to 2010.

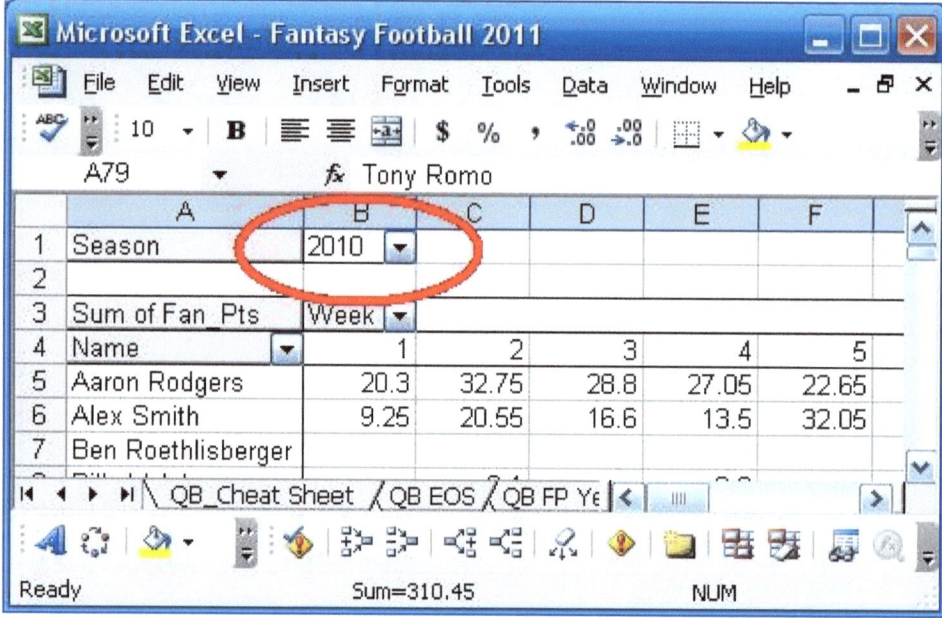

Now, add a Median column to the right of the PivotTable, next to the Grand Total column. Be sure that the Median function only references the weekly fantasy points, and does not include the Grand Total.

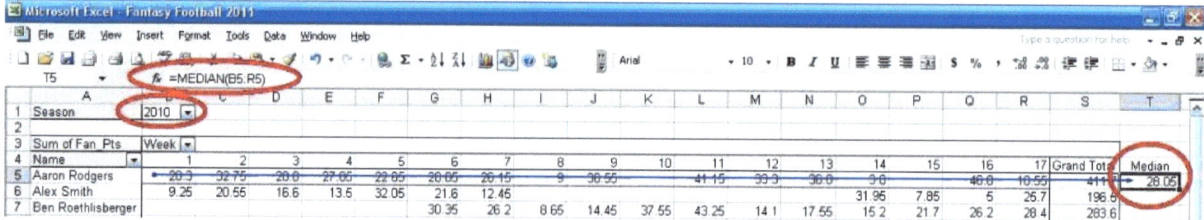

Auto-fill the Median column by double-clicking the fill handle; and your new PivotTable is done!

While we're here, let's rename the worksheet tab to "QB FP Week."

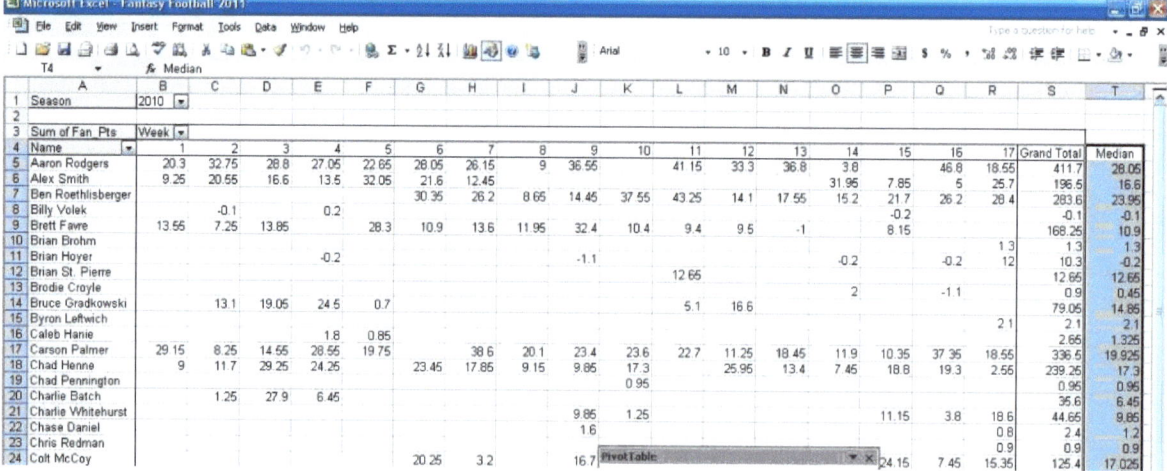

Now, back to our QB Cheat Sheet tab.

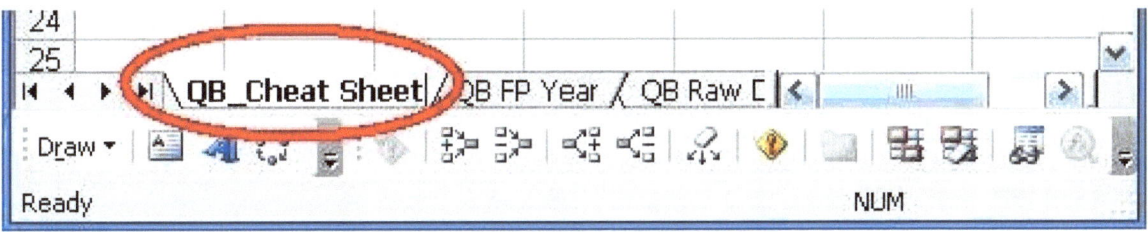

Let's insert a column, titled "Consistency", between the 2010 FP column and the Rank 3 Yr. column.

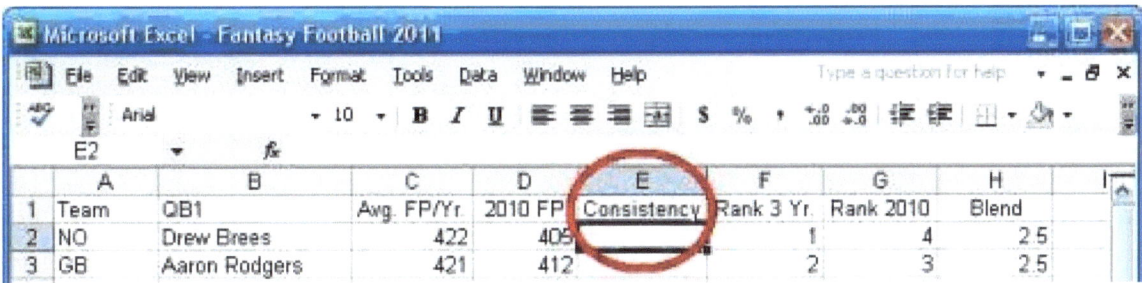

Under the cell labeled "Consistency," insert a VLOOKUP function.

This time, we'll reference the Table_array of the QB FP Week worksheet by highlighting our new PivotTable. (Remember to insert the $'s.)

For Col_index_num, the value of 20 will reference the Median column that we added to the PivotTable.

Enter "FALSE" for the Range_lookup field, since we want exact matches for player names. Click OK.

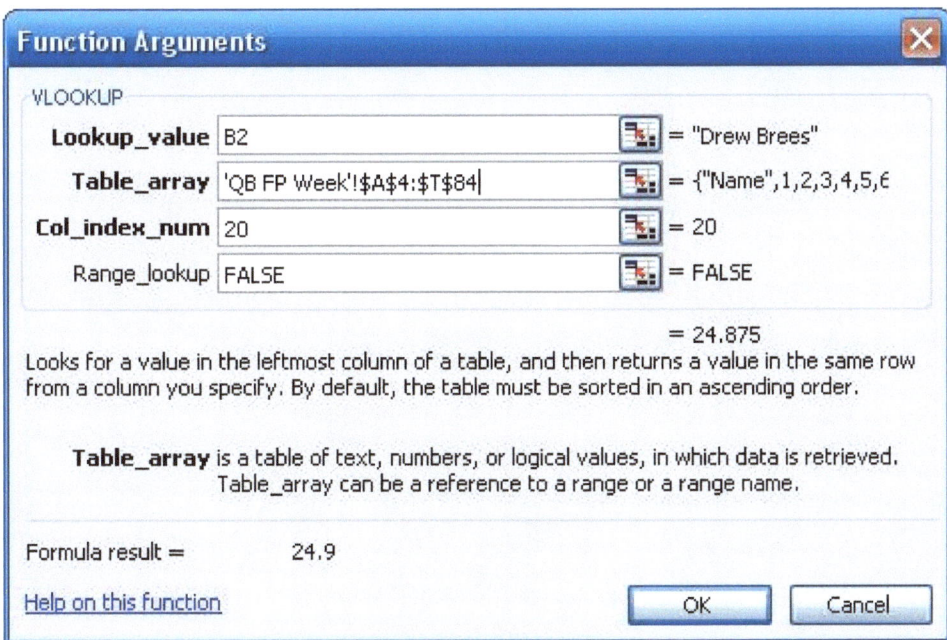

25

Now, let's auto-fill this VLOOKUP function in the Consistency column. I'll again zero out the rookies' "#NA" results.

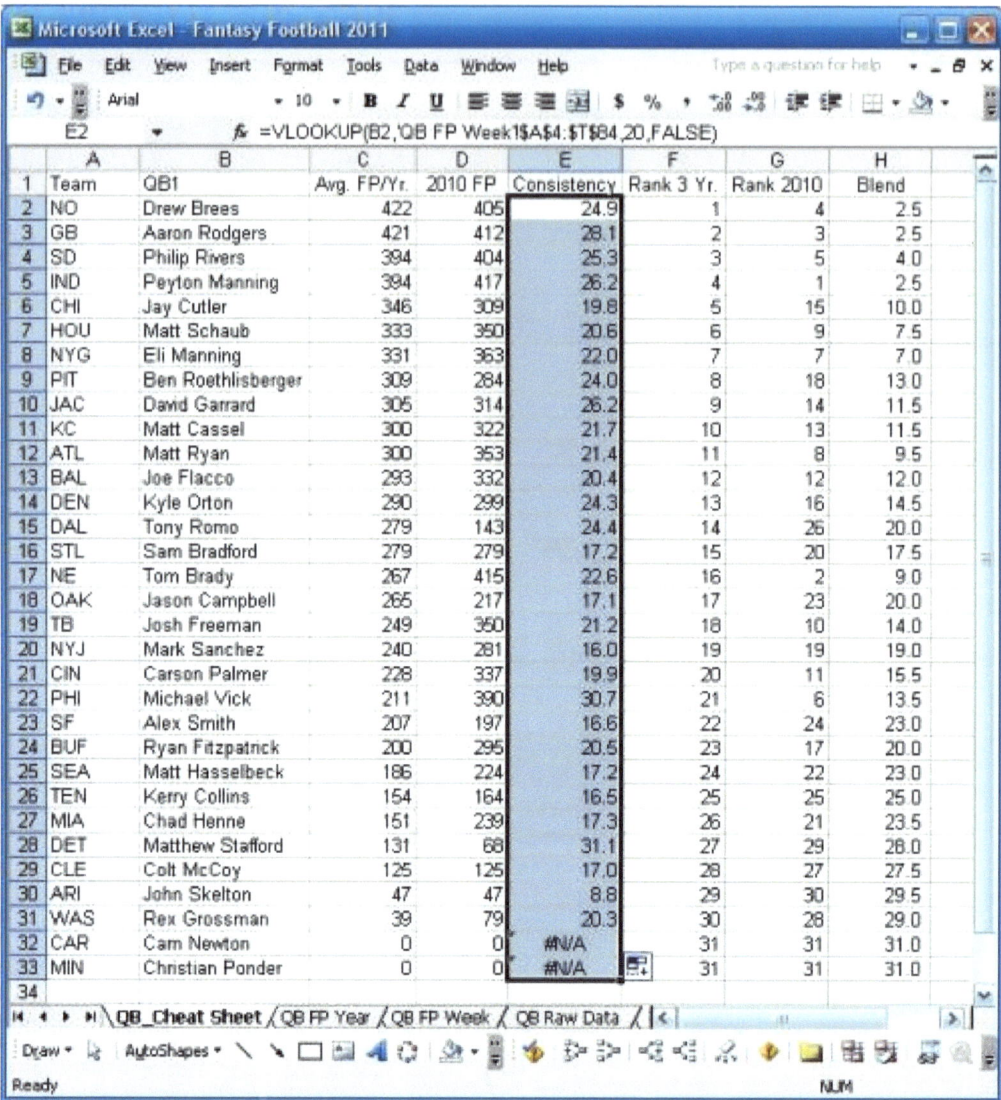

Insert a new column, "Rank Consistency", between the Rank 2010 and Blend columns.

Using the RANK function as we did before, remember to insert "$" as follows; then, auto-fill:

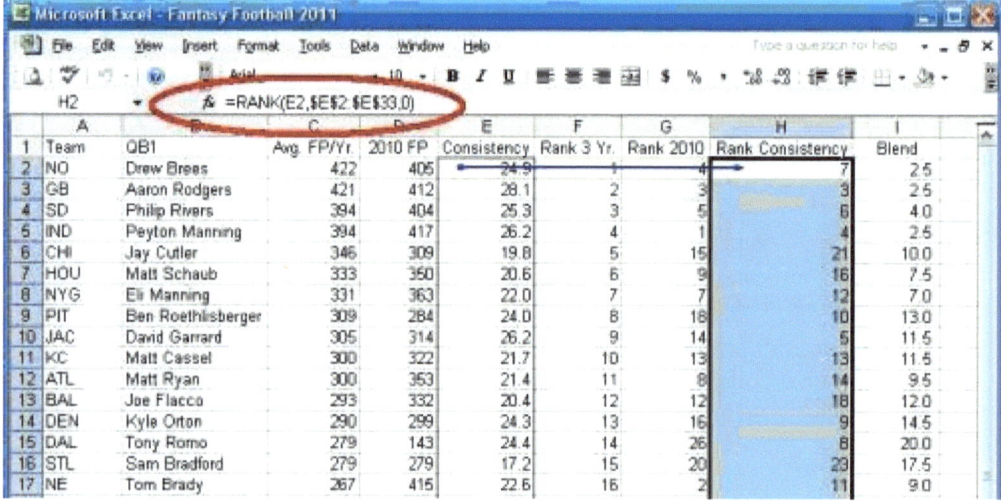

Adjust the Blend column's AVERAGE function to include all three Rank columns: Rank 3 Yr., Rank 2010, and Rank Consistency. Auto-fill this column too.

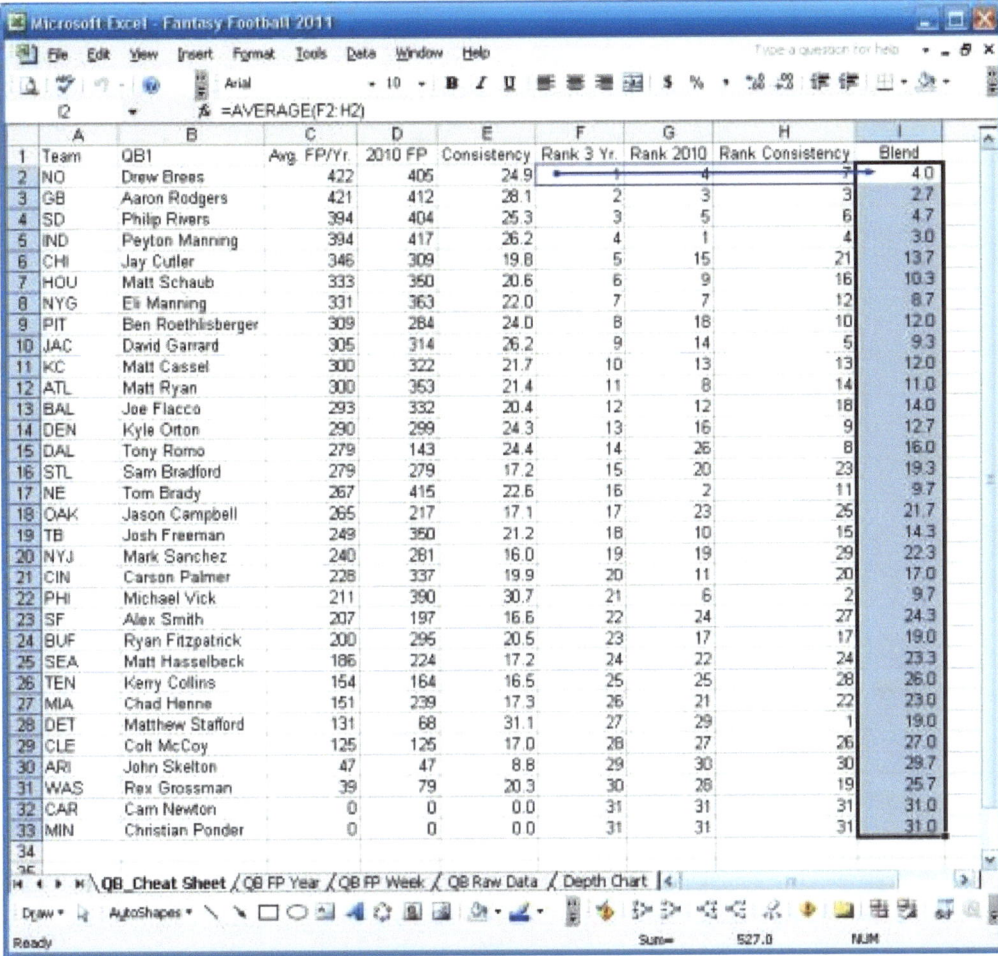

Highlighting the entire table, Sort the table by the Blend column, in Ascending order as follows:

You now have ranked the players by total fantasy point production, and consistency. Furthermore, we have broken our three-way tie for the top rated QB's.

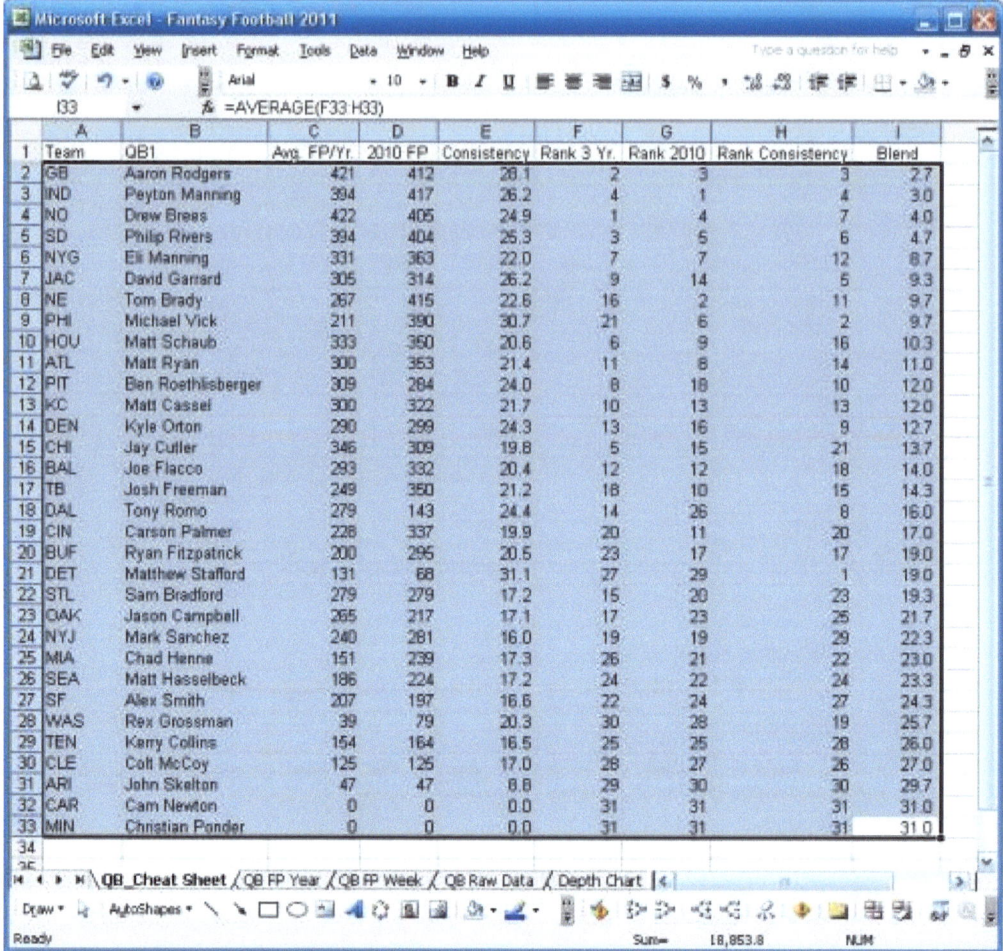

Again, our qualitative judgment may call for us to rank players differently (e.g. Tom Brady and Michael Vick). I'll leave that to your good judgment on draft day.

At this point, I believe that you're now well practiced in using PivotTables and VLOOKUP functions — my primary goal. Way to go!

As I prepare for my own fantasy football draft, I'll add David Dorey's Ease of Schedule and other metrics to my cheat sheet. I'll also implement tiers and dynamic drafting strategies. (By the way, Fantasy Football: The Next Level by David Dorey is an excellent book on improving fantasy football strategy, and definitely one of my favorites.)

Step 8 — Tiers for Fears

Segmenting our cheat sheet by tiers helps us to make decisions quickly during the draft. It simply lumps comparable players together. This gives us an idea of how much fantasy point potential we lose by not drafting the last player available in their tier.

Our blended RANKing (Blend column) accounts for fantasy point potential in the following two ways:

1. Weighted Average of Seasonal Fantasy Points

2. Consistency of Weekly Fantasy Points

Drop-offs in fantasy point potential are usually quite obvious between the 1st and 2nd tiers. Stud players (in this case, A. Rodgers, P. Manning, D. Brees and P. Rivers) tend to outclass everyone else.

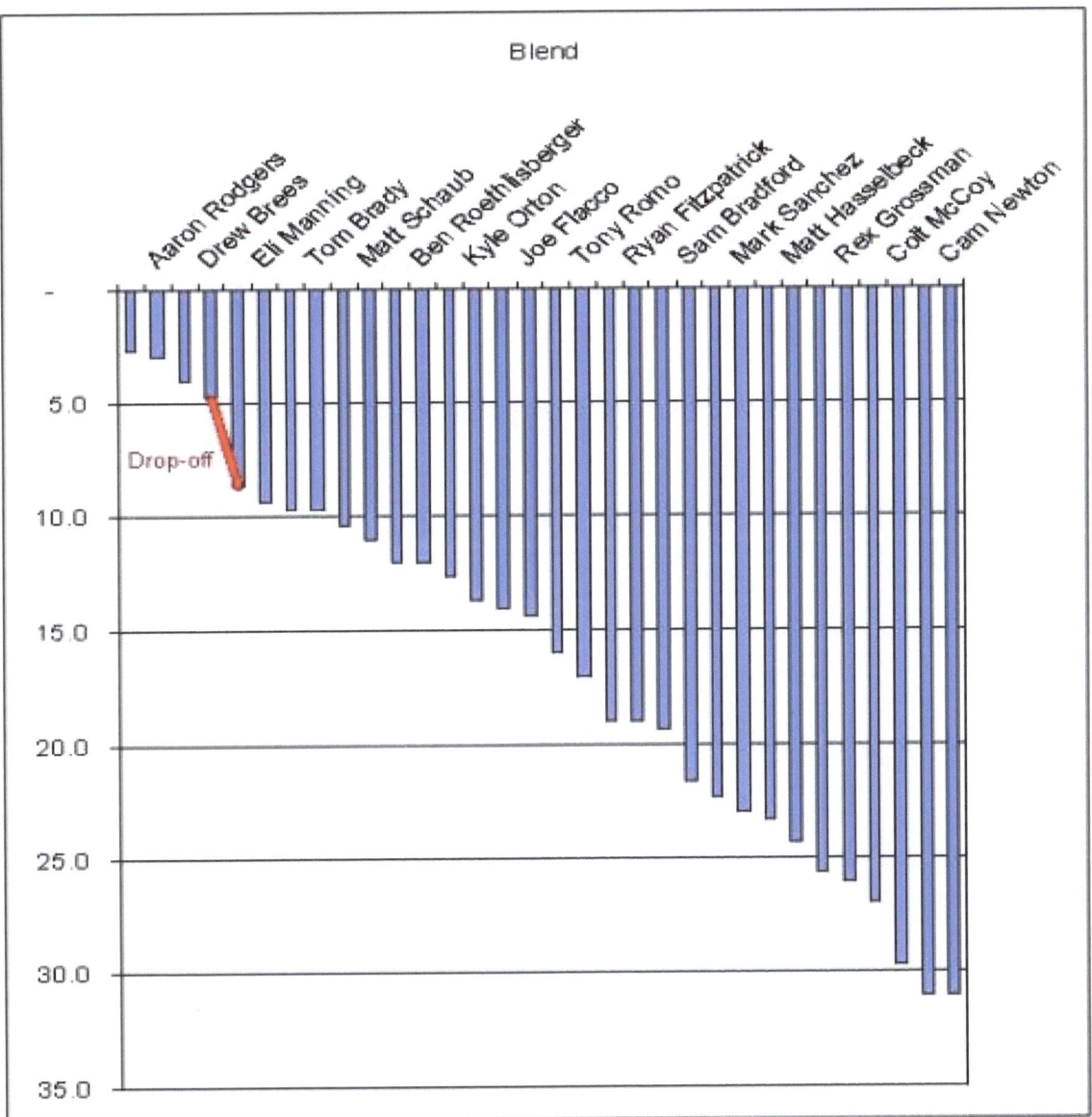

The remaining drop-offs are more subtle. So, we'll need to use quantitative analysis again; but, this one is pretty easy.

Let's begin by measuring the drop-offs by calculating the net difference between each player's blended ranking.

Insert a new column at the end of our cheat sheet, titled "Drop-off." Simply subtract the Blend value of a player from the previous player. Now, auto-fill by double-clicking the fill-handle. (I still love that feature.)

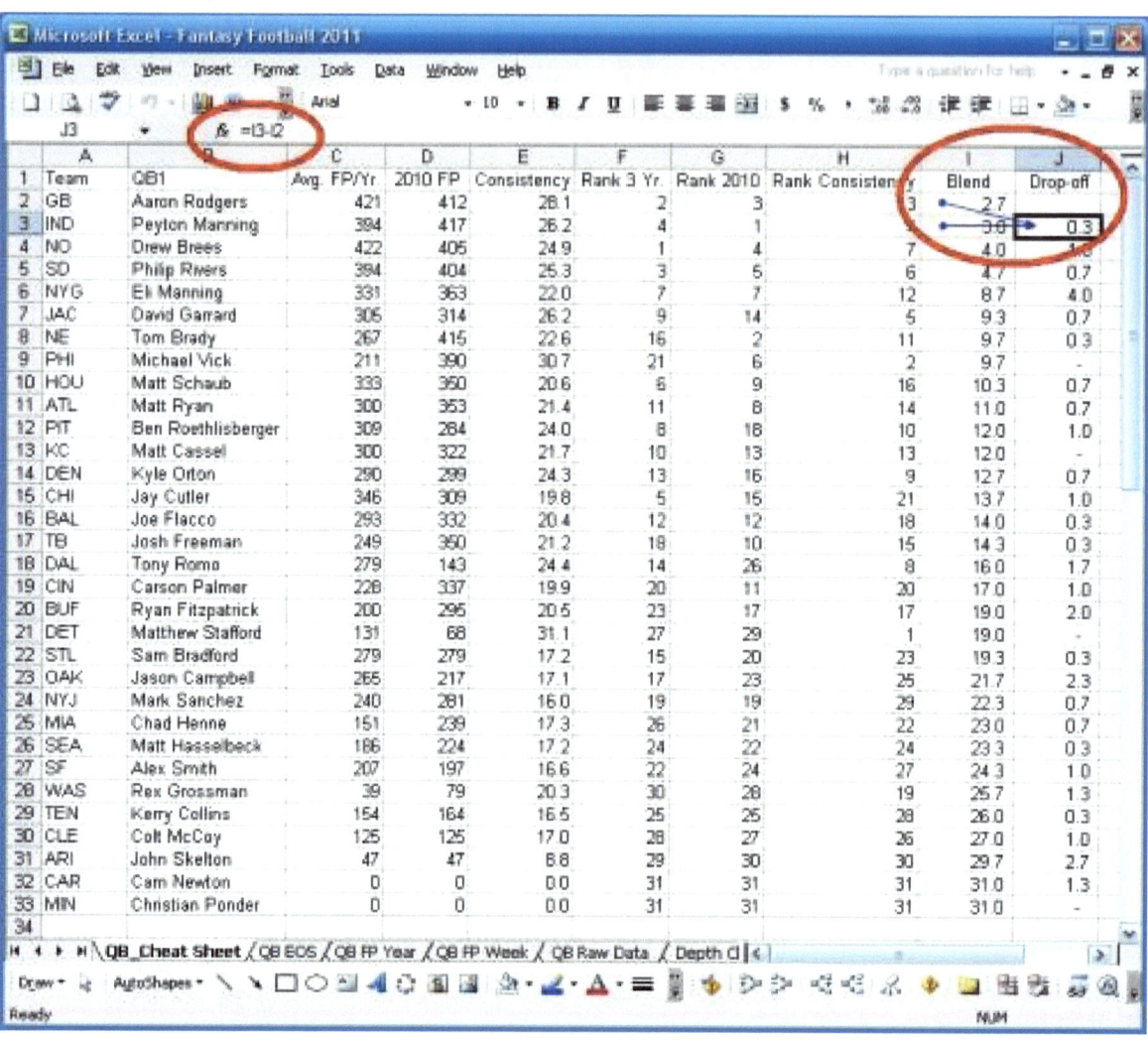

We can now eyeball the next few steepest drop-offs. (It's easy enough that we don't need to use fancy Excel spreadsheet functions.)

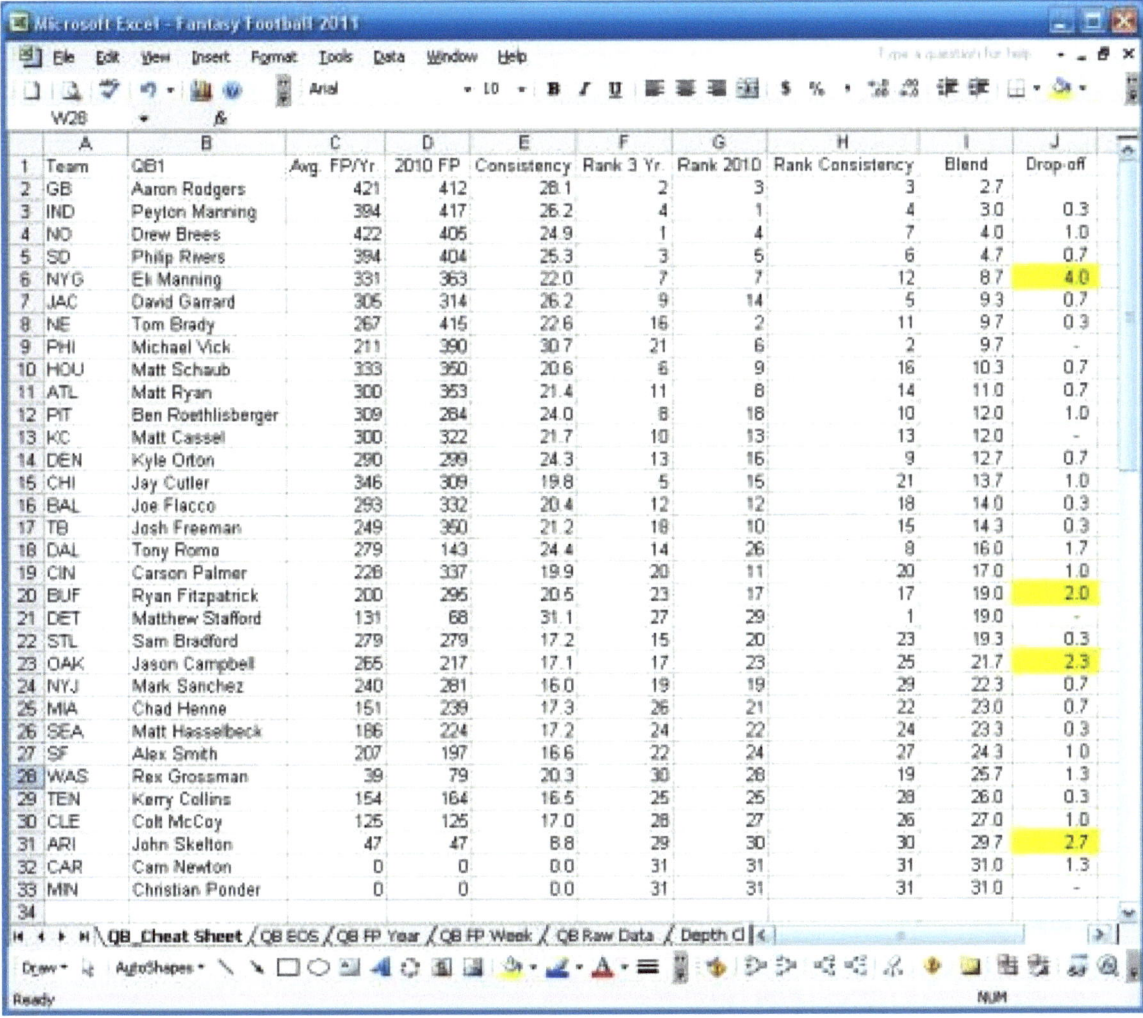

Using our own judgment, we can now categorize players into tiers based on drop-offs.

- Tier 1 (Green) – Studs

- Tier 2 (Gold) – Draft at least one of these players, if you didn't get a stud.

- Tier 3 (Yellow) – Consider these players as backups, if QB's are scarce. Perhaps, pick them up from the waiver wire.

- Tier 4 (White) – Crap

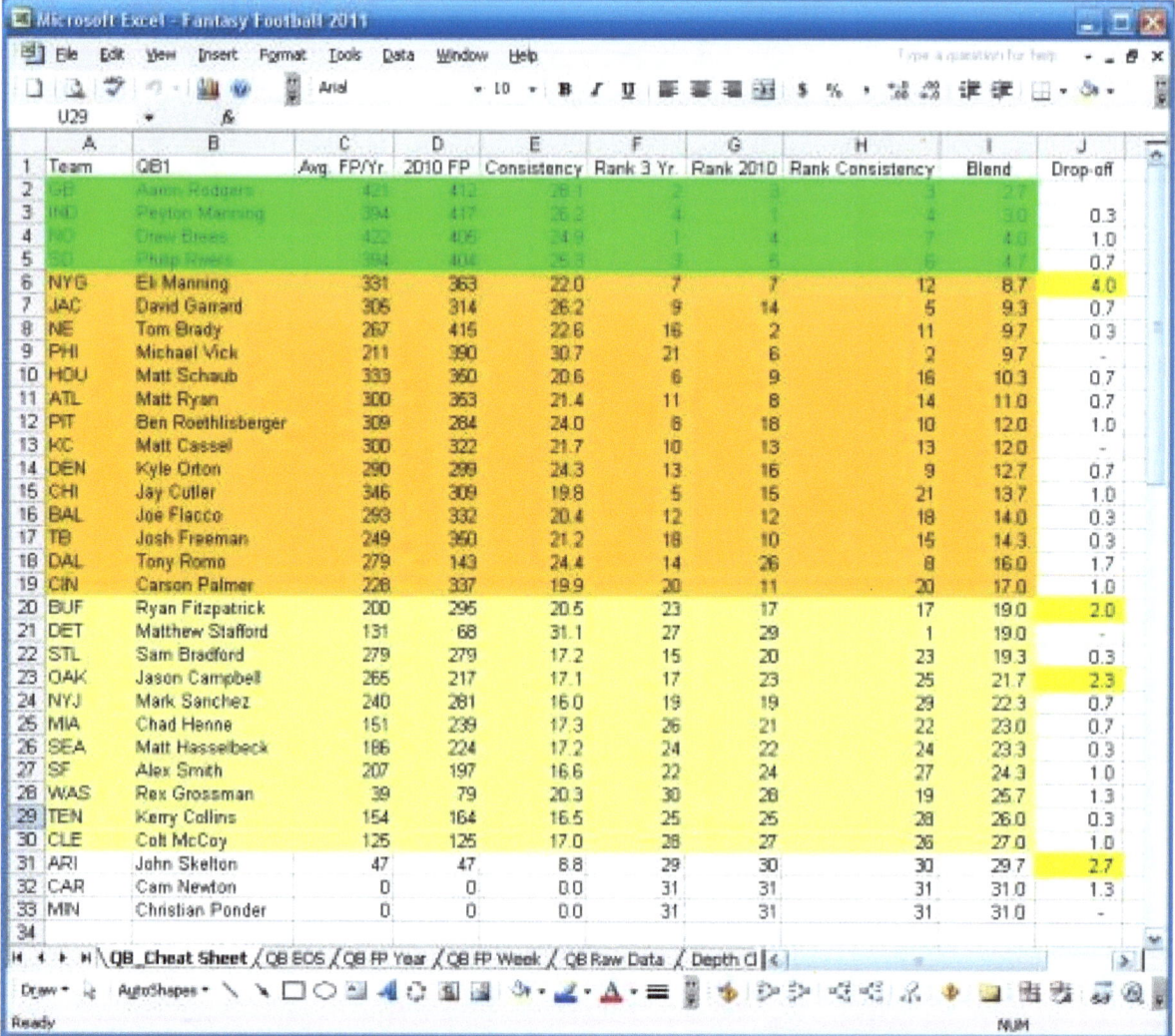

That's it! You have your cheat sheet!

You can apply the same eight steps to other positions too. I apply this process to QB's, RB's and WR's, but not TE's, DEF's or K's. Core positions (QB, RB, WR) generally merit this level of effort, because they consistently produce the most fantasy points. Non-core positions (TE, DEF, K) do not. As a result, I'll often replace my non-core players throughout the season.

Subscribe to my blog (**excelfantasyfootball.wordpress.com**), to automatically get more tools, tips and strategies…and dominate your fantasy football league!

Good luck! Have a good draft! And, have a great season!

www.ingramcontent.com/pod-product-compliance
Lightning Source LLC
Chambersburg PA
CBHW041702160426
43202CB00002B/15